BLENDING PHOTOS WITH FABRIC

a beautiful new way to combine photography, printing and quiltmaking

MARY ELLEN KRANZ & CHERYL HAYES

THE ELECTRIC QUILT COMPANY

Kranz, Mary Ellen
    Blending Photos with Fabric: a beautiful new way to combine photography, printing and quiltmaking
Mary Ellen Kranz and Cheryl Hayes
    p. cm.
ISBN 1-893824-33-0

Published by The Electric Quilt Company
419 Gould Street, Suite 2
Bowling Green, OH 43402 USA

www.electricquilt.com

Printed in Canada

Editor: Penny McMorris
Book and cover design: Jill Hagy
Photography: Mary Ellen Kranz, Cheryl Hayes, Monica Vay
Illustrations: Sara Layne
Editorial assistants: Jenny Novinsky, Andrea Poulimenos, Sara Woodward
Quilt instruction editor: Margaret Okuley

ACKNOWLEDGEMENTS

When we approached writing acknowledgements, we asked ourselves:

Who loves us?

Who encourages us?

Who lets us be ourselves?

Who loves us as ourselves?

Where would we be without girlfriends? Friends?

There are possible quilt images all around you.

From Cheryl:

For me, the answers begin with my family. They are my friends. John and Chandra, who think everything I make is fabulous, Kirstin, who is happy to share a creative eye, and Brent, who just likes to keep me company. Thank you for sharing your life's journey with me.

Friends come in many forms and all are valuable, however, there is something very special about the girlfriends that fill our lives. Mary Ellen is one of mine.

From Mary Ellen:

My husband, Ken, is the answer to all of the questions. Thank you for a lifetime of love, encouragement and support—not to mention bringing the car to a screeching halt so I could take all those pictures. Thank you Andy, Matt, Peter and Natalie for asking and listening and being willing to eat take-out.

Thank you Barb Melchiskey and Marty Bowne—for your deep well of confidence and support. Thank you Judy, Gail, Darlene, Carol, Susan, Kathleen, Paula and Sharon—for your suggestions and enthusiasm. And, thank you, Cheryl, for making it all so much fun.

Keep your eyes open and your camera ready.

Cheryl and Mary Ellen

From Cheryl and Mary Ellen:

Randy Silvers, now an old friend, started it all when he hired both of us to work in his quilt shop (Randy's Quilt Shop in Greensboro, North Carolina). He didn't even fire us when he found out we couldn't work the cash register.

Penny McMorris is a new friend, who sees our creations as something worthy to share with you, our readers and kindred creative spirits.

CONTENTS

ABOUT THE AUTHORS

Mary Ellen Kranz and Cheryl Hayes became friends when they worked together at Randy's Quilt Shop in Greensboro, North Carolina.

Cheryl is a former elementary school teacher who began quilting in 1995. Today she teaches quilting at stores and in her home studio, specializing in color and machine quilting classes. She lives in Charlestown, New Hampshire.

Cheryl Hayes

Mary Ellen Kranz

Mary Ellen has quilted and worked with computers for the past 30 years. She has taught across the country for state and regional guilds and shops as well as at Quilting by the Lake and the International Quilt Festival. She splits her time between homes in North Carolina and Maine.

Together, Mary Ellen and Cheryl run Quilting Images, a mail order service for printed images.

INTRODUCTION

Believe it! If you can write an e-mail, print a letter, or use the Internet, you can create a fabric image on the computer. It's that easy to make your own fabric images. We know, because we've taught hundreds of students to do just that. And an hour into our *Printing Fabric from Your Computer* classes, our students (even those who swore they were computer challenged) were saying:

"I can't believe it. My kids used to laugh at how little I use the computer. Wait until I show them what I can do now."

"Once I got started, I forgot I was working on a computer at all. I was into my picture and imagining the way my finished quilt was going to look."

"You explained this process in plain English and not in the computer jargon I don't understand."

"This is so much more about fabric, color and design than I thought. The computer part of the process was not the central focus. It was just a means to an end."

You'll feel this way too! In this book we'll use terms you already know. We won't let technical stuff get in the way. We'll share our joy of starting with an image, letting that image inspire your quilt, and creating a quilt with your image sewn right in. Your finished quilt will be an original work of art and, no matter what, you will love it because you started with something that excited you in the first place.

Our process for making a photo-inspired quilt has three steps:

1. *Inspiration*—Finding an image of something you love, and letting that image lead the design process
2. *Interpretation*—Getting your image onto washable, lightfast fabric
3. *Creation*—Designing and making quilts that blend your fabric images right into them

Let's get started.

Patten Pond

A lily pond picture can be gotten in any number of ways, and I could have found a lily picture in a book, on a greeting card, or from the Internet. Those pictures may have been beautiful, but they would not have contained the memories of the peaceful morning Ken and I spent sitting quietly at our campsite on the shore of Patten Pond. In the hectic pace of our lives at the time, this was a place where the world stood still for a while. I tried to capture the memory of this peaceful time in the design of this quilt.

- Mary Ellen

Wish We Were There

I was drawn to these postcards in an antique shop because of my love for the beautiful state of Maine. The dates on the cards are from the Depression era—a time my parents spoke of often. The lesson of perseverance by those who lived through that era was passed on to me in their stories. The postcards held their own stories as well. Finding these postcards and reading the notes from one friend to another gave testament to the endurance of friendships—another cherished life lesson!

- Mary Ellen

INSPIRATION

Where do you begin? *Start with something you love.* Think of images that make you take pause in your everyday life. Imagine you are driving. Excluding ice cream and fabric stores, what would you pull over and stop for? Your answers may be varied—wildflowers, sunsets, an old friend, funny signs. All of us come across images that delight our eye and make us smile. These are the stuff of great quilts.

Ask yourself:
What are some of the things that you would pull over and stop to look at? What images could inspire a quilt for you?

The image or images you choose can become the inspiration for your quilt. They will then inspire the mood, color scheme, fabric choices, setting and even the quilting pattern. What's more, when you learn to print these images on fabric, they will even become a part of your quilt.

Here are some of our students' thoughts about this:
"Starting with an image makes the process of choosing fabric for the quilt so much easier. I took the picture and walked around the quilt shop with it. Fabrics just seemed to reach out to me rather than the other way around."

"I was worried about how to place the photo in the quilt, but the photo on my design wall just seemed to draw fabrics to it and pull the quilt along."

"My quilt looks like an Impressionist painting. The photo is in focus and the rest of the quilt just looks like a blurred extension of my picture."

"You told us to try to make it difficult to see where the photo ends and the quilt begins. It's so much fun when people look at my quilt for a while before they even notice that there is an actual photograph in it."

"I'm an avid gardener. I can wrap myself in a quilt with photos of my flowers and enjoy my quilt (and my garden!) all year long."

If your inspiration is a picture waiting to be taken, read on for some tips for successful pictures.

A SHORT GUIDE TO PHOTOGRAPHING YOUR FAVORITE THINGS

Taking pictures is a passion unto itself. Once you start down the road to photo-inspired quiltmaking, you will be amazed at how you see quilt inspiration everywhere. As you look through your camera viewfinder, imagine the scene as a piece of colorful fabric. This is just what it may end up becoming! Look carefully at your subject through the viewfinder. Here are some things to consider before snapping your picture.

The early bird often gets the best picture. This Clematis shot was taken in the early morning. Soft morning, or late afternoon light usually gives you the best color and detail in a photo.

Here's the same Clematis vine, photographed at noon. Notice how the petal and leaf colors look washed out, and you can no longer see the detail of the leaf veins.

Light

Consider the time of day when taking pictures. Time of day can determine light level, influencing the picture's colors. Do you think that good pictures require bright light? Actually, pictures taken in noon sunlight may result in weak, washed-out colors. The **less direct sunlight** of early morning or late afternoon may offer deeper, more true colors. And as an added benefit, you may also get morning dew on flower petals, or interesting shadows cast by a sinking sun.

Shooting morning or late-afternoon pictures can also add shadows to the scene. Sometimes you'll welcome them. In this photo, shadows add strong horizontal stripes across the road; a nice counterpoint to all the vertical tree trunks.

Oops. This striped Clematis is lovely. But look closer. Fully half this photo features mulch. Do we really want to mix mulch-colored fabric in with our greens and pinks? And should we have noticed that green plant stake on the left? We could crop it out if necessary. See page 103.

We did it again—much ado about mulch! Since this photo was taken by shooting down on the iris, the background behind this blue Siberian Iris is mostly mulch. If we had knelt more, to adjust the angle of our shot so green leaves showed behind the flower, we would have more of a blue and green image.

Background

Always check—is the **background appealing** behind your subject? Power lines, passing cars, or signs can be unwanted intruders in your scene. And sometimes mulch, soil or rocks are not the colors you want to incorporate into your quilt. You can adjust some of these things later, in your image editing software, but if you are like us, you'd rather just print and quilt!

Sometimes differences in photos are subtle. Both these flower shots look similar, but notice how one background shows more green, and the other more black and tan. So be sure to watch your background, and perhaps take several shots of any scene you love. Then you can pick and choose.

When Backgrounds Just Aren't Pretty

Sometimes adjusting the angle of the camera shot to get rid of clutter just doesn't accomplish the results we want, so we can take advantage of the **cloning tool** in Paint Shop™ Pro® (or any image editing software). The availability of this is just something to keep in mind when photographing.

*Try though we might, we couldn't photograph this Vermont farm sign without including the wires behind it. Not all of **your** pictures will be perfect either. If you've got to get that special shot, and can't avoid eyesores in the background, take the shot anyway.*

Where did the wires go? We brushed them out using some Clone Brush magic. We'll show you how we did it on page 94.

Area

Imagine the picture you see in your viewfinder as a perfect subject for your photo quilt. Then back up just a bit, or adjust the zoom before snapping. Remember, you may need a **little extra around the edges** for a ¼ inch seam allowance. You'll also want to allow for a bit of shrinkage.

We sure wish we had left more room around this watering can head for our seam allowance.

Surprises

Paying attention now can save time later. Once everything looks perfect and you are ready to snap, check to make sure there are **no finger tips** sneaking in at the edge of the frame. Shoe tips are also common offenders. And, if taking pictures of flowers, be sure you want the surprise guests you will undoubtedly find in your photo. Bees, ladybugs and spiders are always welcome additions!

This insect, ready for his closeup, becomes the star of the photo. He adds needed color (brown, black and orange) and shape to what would other wise be a pretty, but unremarkable shot. Notice the green marigold leaves becoming almost a solid background behind the flowers.

Ready? Aim? Click. Oh, dear, we're all thumbs with this shot. That left-corner blur is an extreme closeup of a finger which got in front of the camera lens.

*This is what the picture on the left **should** have looked like, with no fingers in front of the lens. Some digital cameras today are smaller than a deck of cards, so unless you're careful, fingers can creep into your shot.*

Light Settings for Sunsets

We'll talk more about digital cameras later. But since these cameras can have an overwhelming number of setting choices, we'll say a few words about light settings here. Fortunately, the **automatic** setting works well for most situations. However, at times, a different setting makes a world of difference. We love sunrise and sunset pictures. But since light is dim then, the camera will flash when set on "Auto." This washes out the colors. Use a "Sunset" setting if your camera has one. If not, try shutting off the camera flash.

In certain lights, flash will wash out colors. In this photo the camera is set for auto, and the flash is not turned off. So it automatically flashed in this dim lighting.

The sunset appears more brilliant in this photo. The difference is that no flash was used here. The camera is set for auto, but flash is turned off.

Light Settings for Backlit Scenes

Sometimes a subject simply cannot be captured at the desired angle without the sun shining from behind. If you were to snap the picture under these circumstances, your subject would be dark and indistinguishable. Change the camera setting to "Backlight."

Sun streaming in through a window might be perfect for cat naps, but too bright for pictures. Here Cheryl's cats Brinkley and Maisie appear dark, in contrast with the bright window.

Looks like we changed the camera setting to Backlight just in time. Brinkley is waking up. Notice how the Backlight setting helps throw more light onto our subjects, brightening them.

These two moon pictures were taken one right after another. The only difference between the two is whether flash was used or not. For this picture, the camera was set for auto. But we did not turn the flash off. So when we snapped the picture the camera automatically flashed. The resulting photo only shows us the moon, not the beautiful sky.

Light Settings for Moonlit Scenes

Normally, you think that flash helps in dim light. But look at the moonscapes left and below. They were taken at the same time of night, one right after another. The dark picture (left) is taken at the auto camera setting, and because it was so dark, the camera automatically flashed. The beautiful moon picture (below) is taken with the flash turned off.

For this shot we set the camera on auto, and turned the flash off. When we snapped the picture, we were only using available light. When in doubt about whether or not to use flash, try a shot with both, and see for yourself which you prefer.

Camera Resolution

Consider your digital camera's resolution setting. We like to set our cameras on a high quality resolution. This setting takes more space on your camera memory card, but we feel it is worth the inconvenience. The **high resolution** setting lets you take pictures in a wider frame, and isolate individual items (crop) in the scene later. (See *Tech*nique on page 103 for how to crop.) This ensures you'll have lots of room for making crops of your subject. For example, you may want to crop a single flower out of a garden panorama. If your camera's resolution is set for high, your cropped flower will still be of very good quality.

With images in hand (or in camera), you are ready to move on to the next step—*Interpretation*—which will result in images on fabric!

This one high resolution photo gives us at least four different possible images. All we need to decide is "Is it better like this? Or like this?" While setting your camera on a high quality resolution may result in fewer photos per session (because high-resolution photos take more camera memory), you may get more images per photo (because you can zoom in and pick and choose parts of a photo).

INTERPRETATION

OK—you're inspired! You've got an image. In three more steps you will have that image on fabric.

Step 1: Prepare your fabric to be printed on and become washable and lightfast.

Step 2: Prepare your image to blend into your quilt.

Step 3: Prepare your inkjet printer to produce true images on fabric.

We break the process of getting a photo to fabric into these three steps to simplify it. We've found it makes the process understandable and doable even by computer novices. Our method involves printing your image directly onto a piece of prepared fabric using a computer, software, and an *inkjet* printer. (Note: This is a different process than "photo transfer," which ultimately involves ironing an image onto fabric.) Yes, you can put fabric through your inkjet printer safely. And you'll get excellent results: clear, permanent images on fabric that feels soft.

Let's get started!

STEP 1: PREPARE YOUR FABRIC

In general, there are three routes to take in getting fabric ready to receive your image from an inkjet computer printer—"store-bought," "do-it-yourself," and "mail order." Each way has its own advantages.

Using "Store-Bought" Fabric Sheets

There are several brands of manufactured, ready-for-printing fabric. The fabric has been treated so that the ink used by the various inkjet printers will not separate from the fabric during washing. These store-bought fabrics usually come in packages containing 5-10 sheets. Each sheet has a removable backing (sometimes called a "carrier" because this backing "carries" the fabric through the printer.) The most common sheet size is the same as a sheet of printer paper—8$\frac{1}{2}$ x 11 inches. Some brands offer other sheet sizes as well, or even a roll of fabric—perfect for scarves or banners.

Keep "store-bought" fabric sheets in their original package so they stay flat and dry. And be sure to read the package instructions. Each brand's post-printing treatment will vary. See more tips, on shrinkage and light protection, starting on page 26.

The fabric in the store-bought packages is usually high-thread-count white or cream cotton. Several brands also offer a range of cotton weights such as sheeting or twill as well as silk.

It is extremely important to read and follow the post-printing directions for the particular fabric sheet brand you are using. These instructions, on how to treat the fabric once it has been put through the printer, may differ widely from brand to brand. For example, some require heat-setting the printed piece with an iron. For others, this step has no effect.

Our students have pointed out some little differences between brands that you may want to be aware of:

"The brand I purchased had diagonal trim cuts across each corner. This seemed to prevent my printer from jamming as the fabric sheet started through."

If the brand you choose doesn't have this feature, get out your scissors and snip the square corners off.

"Even though they both said the color was white, I liked one brand better than the other because it was a brighter white."

"One of the brands I used was a bit stiff to the touch. I tried another and it was much softer."

Be sure you test print your image on paper (and know which side of the paper gets printed on) before putting one of your precious fabric sheets into the printer.

It turned out that the brand that was the whitest was also the stiffest. If these kinds of differences are important to your project, you may need to experiment. Try a couple different brands to find the one that looks and feels best to you.

Once you settle on a favorite brand, be sure to purchase enough for your entire project. Because printers don't print white, if you use fabric sheets with different base colors, your photo images can appear to be from different dye lots in the finished pieces.

Cost can be the deciding factor in whether you use packaged printer fabrics or treat and prepare your own. Generally, pre-treated sheets cost around $1.50 to $3.00 per sheet (or somewhat less when purchased in quantity). At first glance, this can seem pricey, especially if you are new to the process and not sure of your computer printing skills. Mess-ups (now there's a technical term!) can be costly. So it really pays to test-print your image first on paper before printing on your fabric sheet.

Even if you decide to prepare your own fabric for printing, it is nice to have a package of prepared sheets on hand. You never know when you will have a burning desire to immediately print an image, or need a fabric sheet to print a last minute label for a gift quilt. You can't always afford the time the "do-it-yourself" method takes. So having a few sheets ready to go can be a real lifesaver.

Making "Do-It-Yourself" Fabric Sheets

We use a clear liquid called Bubble Jet Set 2000 to make our own ready-to-print fabric sheets. We always tell students in our *Printing Fabric from Your Computer* class that we will cover a range of topics, from the sublime to the ridiculous, but it will all be fun and exciting. For example, the process for preparing your own fabric begins with dipping white fabric into clear liquid and hanging it on the line. However ridiculous this process seems, it's always fun. And it works! The fabric you end up with will be washable after it has been printed on with an inkjet computer printer.

The chart on the following page tells you what materials you need to prepare **four sheets** of your own fabric for printing.

To make our own ready-to-print fabric sheets we soak strips of 100% cotton fabric in Bubble Jet Set 2000 solution for 5 minutes, making sure all parts of the fabric get saturated by the liquid. See our full instructions, beginning on this page.

How to Treat Your Fabric with Bubble Jet Set 2000

1. Lightly fold your ⅓ yd. fabric strip to fit into a container such as a plastic dishpan or glass baking pan.

2. Place the fabric in your container.

3. Pour the Bubble Jet Set 2000 on the fabric.

4. Turn the folded fabric over several times to be sure it is saturated. (Bubble Jet Set 2000 is reusable. If you have some left in the pan you can pour it back into the bottle when you are finished.)

5. Let soak for 5 minutes.

6. Hang the fabric on the line or drying rack to dry. If you are in a big hurry, you can use a hair dryer on the low setting to speed the process.

7. When dry, iron your fabric strip.

After soaking the fabric in Bubble Jet Set 2000 for 5 minutes and hanging their fabric strips on the line to air dry, a group of students at Quilting by the Lake have just finished an important part of Step 1 (Prepare your Fabric). In our classes, two hands raised in the air indicate a "Teaching Moment." A little spoof, we think, on the teacher!

Material	How Much	Notes
High thread count, 42 inch wide cotton fabric	1/3 yd.	For your first project, you may want to use a white or near white pima or other high quality cotton fabric. Some local quilt shops (and internet sites) carry a range of cotton fabric suitable for inkjet printing. Some fabrics are designated PFD – prepared for dyeing. We have used both PFD and other high quality cotton and not found any appreciable difference. You do not need to pre-wash or iron your fabric.
Bubble Jet Set 2000	1/3 cup	This clear liquid, made by the C. Jenkins Necktie & Chemical Company, can be purchased at many local quilt shops or via the Internet in 18 or 32 oz. bottles. Complete instructions are on the label.

Backing to which the fabric will be adhered while going through the printer		Choose one of these for your backing:
		    A) Self-Adhesive Template Sheets
		    B) Full Sheets of Label Paper
		    C) Freezer Paper Sheets
		See details of each below.

A) Self-Adhesive Template Sheets	4	These 8 1/2 x 11 inch thin vinyl sheets are sold in packages of 10 and make an ideal backing for our fabric sheets. You peel the paper backing off and adhere the sturdy but flexible sticky-backed sheets to your prepared fabric. These sheets stick readily to the fabric and yet are relatively easy to pull off when you are finished printing. They can be re-used several times as well.
B) Full (8 1/2 x 11 inch) Sheets of Label Paper	4	Your office supply store carries packages of label paper meant to go through an inkjet computer printer. The "full sheet" type of label paper makes an almost perfect carrier on which your fabric can ride through your printer. You peel the label backing off and use the label itself, which is quite sticky, to provide a stiff back for your fabric. Your fabric will not peel off easily which is an advantage while you are printing but requires a special technique (described on page 26) when you are finished and ready to release your printer fabric from the label.
OR		OR
C) Freezer Paper Sheets	4	Flat sheets of freezer paper, cut 8 1/2 x 11 inches, are good fabric carriers. While less expensive than label sheets, freezer paper sheets can separate from the fabric on their ride through the printer. Flatten the paper you cut from a roll first or use the heavier weight freezer paper sheets that are packaged and sold just for this application. Either way, ironing the paper onto the fabric slowly with high heat is key. We'll talk about this later.
Protective gloves	1 pair	The Bubble Jet Set 2000 label says to use these.
Container to soak fabric	1	A clean plastic dishpan or an old glass baking pan works fine.
Clothes line or drying rack	1	Clean the line or drying rack off where you will be hanging your white fabric. If your drying rack is made of wood, use paper towels under the fabric to keep the wood oils from bleeding through.
Rotary cutter with sharp blade, cutting mat, and ruler		You will cut your fabric sheet out *after* you have adhered the backing to it.

Adding Backing Sheets

Your fabric is soft, and can't feed through your printer by itself. So you need to back the fabric with something stiff enough to carry it through your printer. Self-adhesive Template Sheets or label paper (with the sticky stuff on the back) both make good backing sheets.

Using the Template Sheets or the full sheet label paper:

1. Lay your fabric strip out on a table (right side down, if there is a right side), making sure it is flat and smooth.

2. Peel the backing paper off the Template Sheet or label paper. Dispose of the backing.

3. Hold the template or label sheet over your fabric strip and gently place it sticky side down on the fabric. The long edge of the paper should be parallel to the selvage edges of the fabric. Leave a little fabric around all sides of the paper.

4. With your hands, gently pat the Template Sheet or label paper onto the fabric.

5. Carefully move your template or label paper/fabric strip (paper side up) to your cutting table.

Adding Backing Sheets Using Freezer Paper

Using $8^{1}/_{2}$″ x 11″ sheets of freezer paper (either sheets you cut yourself, or pre-cut sheets available to buy):

1. Lay your fabric strip on your ironing board, making sure it is flat and smooth.

2. Place a sheet of freezer paper, shiny side down, over one end of your fabric strip. The long edge of the paper should be parallel to the selvage edges of the fabric.

3. With your dry iron set to high, press the freezer paper slowly and with some pressure onto your fabric. Don't rush this step—you want the paper to stick especially well at the edges of the sheet.

4. Carefully move your freezer paper/fabric strip (paper side up) to your cutting table.

Cutting Out Your Fabric Sheet

1. On your cutting table, use your rotary cutter, mat and ruler to cut your fabric exactly at the edges of the paper. *It is very important that there be **no extra fabric**—not even a tiny bit—extending out from the carrier sheet. It is better to cut off a bit of the paper along with the fabric than to leave a little bit of fabric showing around the paper.*

2. Snip a small ($^{1}/_{8}$ inch) diagonal cut across each corner of your fabric sheet. This will help the sheet get going smoothly through the printer.

By repeating these steps, you should have four fabric sheets ready to go through your inkjet printer.

Once our fabric strips are dry, we iron them and lay them on the cutting table. Each 9″ strip of fabric yields four $8^{1}/_{2}$″ x 11″ fabric sheets. You'll notice the lint roller at the ready. Just before inserting the fabric into the printer we like to lightly roll the lint remover over it. This insures that there are no stray threads which could interfere with the application of printer ink on our fabric sheet. We use our Fabric Sheet Trimmer to cut out a perfect $8^{1}/_{2}$″ x 11″ sheet. See page 29.

OUR STUDENTS ALWAYS ASK:

"How many sheets can I prepare at a time? Can I stockpile the sheets I make using Bubble Jet Set 2000 so I have them ready when needed?"

A: The official answer (from the bottle label) is to prepare your fabric sheets and use them "immediately." We didn't know this when we first started, so we made several dozen sheets at one time. We stored them in plastic zip bags and used them over the course of about six months. We didn't notice any problems at all. Again, the manufacturer's directions do say to use your treated fabric shortly after treating with Bubble Jet Set 2000.

"If there are little threads along the edges of my backed fabric sheets, do I just pull them off?"

A: No. Snip them off with a thread snip or small scissors instead. Also, make sure the fabric surface is free of little threads and other thread "schnibbles." These are not good for your printer's digestion! Additionally, your printer might carry these thread particles right along and print over them. When you brush them off later, there will be white specks on your fabric photo where the ink didn't get to the surface.

"Should I re-iron my fabric sheets that have freezer paper backing just before putting them through the printer?"

A: Yes. We always give the freezer-paper-backed fabric sheets one final going over with the iron— particularly the leading edge that will go into the printer first. (We never iron the Template Sheet or label-paper-backed fabric sheets, however.)

"Any other tips on handling freezer-paper-backed fabric sheets?"

A: Handle your fabric sheets tenderly on the way to the printer. At this point, they should be well adhered to the backing and lint and thread free. Avoid folding or over-handling them so they are still intact when you put them into the printer feed area. When we use freezer paper backing, we sometimes give the leading edge of the sheet (the edge that goes into the printer first) a little extra pressing with the iron.

"Can I reuse freezer paper?"

A: While you can sometimes re-use your freezer paper sheets, we don't recommend it unless you are using the heavier weight freezer paper sheets. Even then, you may find they don't adhere as well after two or three uses.

"Can I reuse label paper?"

A: Yes. Label paper gets a bit better with age. At first, it is much more difficult to remove from the fabric. But it gets its groove about three times through the process. We've re-used label paper backing five or six times with no problems in having the paper attached to the fabric while going through the printer.

"When and how do I remove the backing from the fabric?"

A: The Bubble Jet Set 2000 directions say to let the printed fabric sheets rest for 30 minutes after printing. Template Sheets and freezer paper will pull off easily once you get a corner to release from the fabric. Label paper backing, however, needs a special touch. To remove the label paper:

1. Carefully peel about ½″ of the label paper from the top or bottom edge of the fabric.

2. Stick the exposed, sticky edge of the label to the edge of a table or counter so that the fabric side is toward the back.

3. Reach around both sides of the hanging fabric sheet. Grab the corners of the fabric that have been separated from the label.

4. Slowly pull the fabric straight down until it is completely free of the label. The fabric may roll up at this point, but a light touch with the iron will flatten it out.

5. Un-stick the label paper from the edge of the table or counter and, if it's still tacky and intact, save for reuse.

"Do I need to allow for shrinkage?"

A: Yes. To be on the safe side, always plan to print your image about ¼″ larger on all four sides. Then trim to fit after you've post-treated the fabric following the manufacturer's instructions.

"Can I use my printer fabric sheet right away, or should I wash it first?"

A: The directions on the bottle of Bubble Jet Set 2000 are very specific about post-treating the fabric. This post-treatment is important, as it activates the process for making your fabric washable. See the suggestions on the following page from the company that manufactures Bubble Jet Set 2000.

How do I keep my printed fabric looking as good as when it came out of the printer? What is the difference between Post Treatment, Washing and Light Protection?

A: **Post Treatment:**
Whether you treat your own fabric with Bubble Jet Set 2000 or use pre-packaged fabric sheets, you'll find instructions included for "post-treating" your inkjet printed fabric images after they come out of the printer. These vary by manufacturer and are critical to the process of preserving your prints.

1. Always read and carefully follow the specific instructions provided by the manufacturer regarding post-treatment of your inkjet-printed piece. Each manufacturer's instructions will differ, and these methods will be different still from the post-treatment for Bubble Jet Set 2000 treated fabric sheets.

2. Check the manufacturer's website periodically for updates and changes. Recently, for example, the Bubble Jet manufacturer website (http://www.cjenkinscompany.com) published a list of HP printers that will not work with BJS.

Washing:

While today's products for printing and preserving printed images on fabric give far superior results than those of just a year or two ago, they certainly do not hold up to washing as well as most commercially printed fabric. At this time, you should expect some color loss when you wash your inkjet fabric printed sheets. The amount of color loss will differ depending on a variety of factors. To minimize color loss, here are some procedures we follow regarding washing:

1. Wash using lots of water and minimal agitation. We don't want our printed fabrics to rub against other fabrics if possible. Use a short cycle and check periodically to see that the printed pieces are not folded over against each other.

2. Use a very mild washing agent. Bubble Jet Rinse (a bit of a misnomer as it is a washing agent not a rinse) is recommended by the makers of Bubble Jet Set.

3. Line or lay flat to dry your piece away from direct sunlight.

Many of our pieces are wallhangings, not intended to be washed regularly. Therefore, we did not wash our printed fabric sheets prior to incorporating them in these quilted pieces. In those pieces meant to be used as quilts, we washed the entire quilt just after it was completed, following the above guidelines. The pictures in these quilts are not as brilliant as those in our wallhangings. But they're still very beautiful to us. The color loss seemed to vary more by hue than anything else, with red and black seeming to lose the most brilliance.

Light Protection:

Bright light, particularly sunlight, will fade your inkjet-printed pieces over time. Printers that use so-called "archival" ink are said to provide a measure of lightfastness (see page 38). If your printer does not use these inks (and even if it does), we recommend spraying your finished piece with a product such as Fabric Shield or Quiltgard™. These do not appear to harm the look or feel of the finished quilted piece and are said to protect from UV rays. It is wise to re-spray your piece after washing or several months of light exposure.

Again, stay abreast of the latest information on these issues. Products and processes to aid us in this creative adventure are coming along to make our work more long-lasting. We already know how to make it beautiful!

Here is specific use information about Bubble Jet Set 2000 from the manufacturer:

BUBBLE JET SET 2000

A letter for all Bubble Jet Set 2000 users from company President Jerome Jenkins:

I am writing this letter to all crafters because there is a lot of incorrect information out there about how to use this product.

1 If you are using or selling the Original Bubble Jet Set formula please tell all consumers that this product has been replaced with the Bubble Jet Set 2000.

2 The Bubble Jet Set 2000 will work with HP printers and all other printers.* This product replaced the original formula—we do not manufacture the original formula any longer.

3 This product cannot be heat set. If you attempt to heat set this product it will not work at all! Many crafters attempt to make the image permanent by heating in the dryer or with an iron. The final step—washing the fabric with a mild detergent—is necessary in making this product work correctly.

4 This product only works with 100% cotton or 100% silk. If you use fabrics with synthetic blends, it will not work.

5 Results will vary with different printers.

6 DO NOT WASH IN COLD WATER ONLY! You must use a mild detergent when washing the fabric. We highly recommend the Bubble Jet Rinse product. If you do not wash your designs with a mild detergent, it will BLEED! The purpose for this step is to get the loose inks out of the fabric. Cold water will not get these loose inks out of the fabric and when it dries it will bleed! If washing the fabric by hand, please wash with the Bubble Jet Rinse and work the rinse in the fabric for about 2 minutes. This should get all the loose inks out. Again, do not simply run the fabric under cold water.

7 Most important—please follow the instructions on the bottle!

*Editor's note: See www.cjenkinscompany.com for a list of HP printers that will not work with Bubble Jet Set 2000

Mail Order Services for Printed Images

If you want someone to print your photos onto fabric for you, there are services that will do this. You send your photos via e-mail or regular mail along with your specifications (such as size and quantity).

One such service is Quilting Images (owned and operated by us: Mary Ellen and Cheryl). Quilting Images stays abreast of the latest products and techniques and offers printing services on a variety of fabrics (cotton, silk, canvas, etc.). We can print images in large sizes as well.

Quilting Images also can provide you with images to print, from a vast selection of original images. You can choose images to print on fabric yourself or QI will print them for you.

You can reach Quilting Images by visiting the web site: **www.quiltingimages.com** or by regular mail at:

**Quilting Images
P.O. Box 305
Charlestown, New Hampshire 03603-0305**

Fabric Sheet Trimmer

We have developed a special ruler called the Quilting Images Fabric Sheet Trimmer to use when cutting our treated fabric sheets around the edges of an $8\frac{1}{2}$ by 11 inch backing. Complete with "glowing" edges, the trimmer allows you to be sure that there isn't any extra fabric extending beyond the backing and helps to minimize fraying. This ruler is available at www.quiltingimages.com.

Send us your photos or we'll send you ours. Our Web site, www.quiltingimages.com tells you what services we offer. We'll custom print your own photographs for you onto fabric. Or you can browse through photographs we've taken and choose images to print on fabric yourself. You can also see where we're offering classes. Come visit us!

STEP 2: PREPARE YOUR IMAGE

Okay. You've got your inspiration image. Now you need to get that photo/image onto fabric, so it can become not just the *inspiration for*, but *a part of* your quilt. To do that, you need to get your image into the computer and, if necessary, adjust your image.

Getting Your Image into the Computer

Think of your computer as a house with numerous doors through which images might enter and exit. Scanners, digital cameras, CD and floppy drives, the keyboard, and your Internet connection are all entrance doors, letting images in. Your printer is an exit door, letting images out.

The table on the opposite page suggests the kinds of images you may choose to work with, and what "door" you would use to get them into the computer.

Once Inside, Where Does Your Image Go?

Let's assume for the moment that the image has made it through one of the "doors" of your computer. Where will it go now? The image goes where you put it. Again, from one of our students,

"I have no trouble scanning my pictures into the computer. I just can't remember where I put them!"

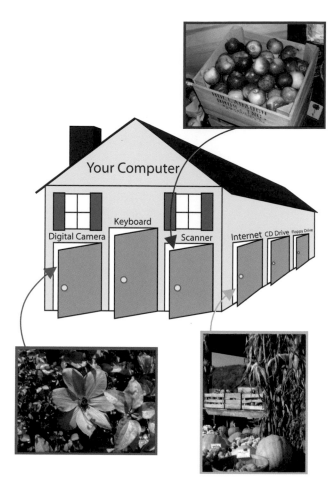

Think of your computer as a house. To get images into this "house" you use "doors." Think of these doors as equipment or software which can bring images into your "house."

Possible Images	"Doors" into Your Computer
• Photographs (the printed-on-paper kind) • Letters, poems, or text passages on paper • Children's drawings • 3-dimensional objects (e.g., shells, leaves) • Maps and charts	Scanner
• Images of places you've been, people you find interesting, or things you love...	Digital camera
• Images saved on CDs (e.g. the kind you can get when processing a roll of film) • Images saved on floppy disks	Graphics software
• Images attached to e-mail messages • Images downloaded from web sites	Internet software
• Stories, poems, letters you compose on computer	Word processing software
• Images created with software on your computer	Graphics software

You need to **assign a place you'll remember.** Continuing our house analogy, let's say that every time you bring an image into the computer, you send it to a certain room—one that will hold all of your images. In computer speak, this is called a folder. *If you establish right at the beginning that all incoming images will go into a particular folder, then you will know exactly where to go when you want to work with your image and print it out.* In other words, decide which room to put your images into in your house. Then you'll always know where to find them.

Now where did my photos go?

It's easy to lose things in your real house, and just as easy to lose images in your computer. To make it easy to find your images again inside your computer, keep them all in one special place (folder).

How to Set up a Special Folder (Room) to Hold All Your Images

We'll assume you are using a PC and running the Windows XP operating system. (If you have a different make or model, don't worry—the concept is what is important. In that case you would follow the steps in your particular computer's help files for how to create a new folder—one that you would use for your images.) The idea is that **you want a single place** (room) to put your images, and that **you will remember the name** of that place (which room it is) when you need to find your images again.

1. Right-click any blank area on your computer desktop (main screen). A menu appears.

2. Point to New, then click Folder. A folder icon labeled *New Folder* on a blue background should appear on the desktop.

3. Immediately type a name for your image folder. We used *Joyful Images* for this folder name. (If you wind up with *New Folder* as the name of your folder before you get to type, just right-click the new folder icon, click Rename and type a name for your image folder here.) You should now have a folder icon on the desktop, ready and waiting to store your images.

The important concept here is that **you now have a place to store your images** as they come into your computer, from whatever door (scanner, camera, Internet etc.) you use.

Step 1

Step 2

Step 3

Using Paint Shop™ Pro® to Prepare Your Image

We use Paint Shop™ Pro® as our image editing software. Let's use it here to get your picture ready to print on the printer. If you have other graphics software, the steps may vary although the concepts are transferable.

1. Open Paint Shop™ Pro®. (Our instructions work with Paint Shop™ Pro® 8 or higher.)

2. Click the **Browse** button.

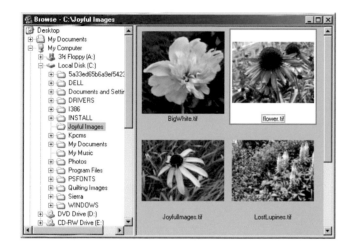

3. Drag the scroll button down until you see your folder name.

4. Click the folder containing your pictures.

5. Click your picture name, to select your picture.

6. Double-click on your picture name, to open your picture.

With your picture on the computer screen, let's improve it, using Paint Shop™ Pro's® automatic **Enhance Photo** function.

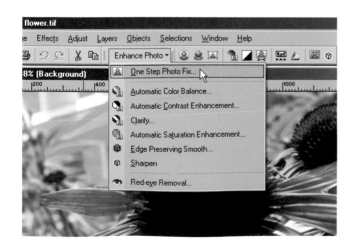

7. Click the words **Enhance Photo** on the menu bar. A menu drops down.

8. Click **One Step Photo Fix**.

Notice that the software automatically makes your picture sharper and balances the color.

If you do not like what the software automatically does to your picture, you can undo the change by clicking EDIT on the main menu bar and then clicking **Undo**.

Paint Shop™ Pro® has a way to print that allows you to position your picture (or several pictures, if you open more than one) on a page. Instead of choosing **Print** under the FILE menu, let's choose **Print Layout**.

9. Click FILE on the main menu bar—click **Print Layout**.

The Print Layout function will let you move the picture on a screen version of your fabric sheet. You can even adjust the photo size to the real size you need for your quilt. Let's do it.

10. Click your picture, showing at the left of your screen. Holding down your left mouse button, drag the picture to the blank page. (Your blank page may show a grid. It's okay if it does.) Your picture will pop onto the page. Note: If you get a message "This image will not fit on the paper without scaling it. Do you wish to scale it?" click Yes. You do want to rescale it.

11. Click one of the solid black squares at the corner of the picture and drag the mouse diagonally in and out to resize the image. Notice that as you resize the image, the exact picture size appears in the lower-right of the screen.

Click and drag any black square to rescale.

12. Click the center of the picture and drag the mouse to move the picture on the page.

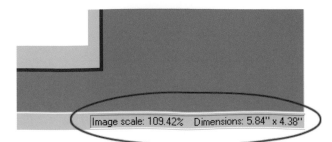

STEP 3: PREPARE YOUR PRINTER

Before you print, get your printer ready to print on fabric by changing some printer settings.

Printing Tips

- Let your printed fabric sheet rest for 30 minutes before removing the backing.
- Use only the ink and cartridges recommended by the printer manufacturer.
- Every so often, run your printer's maintenance software. It takes just a few minutes, and does some handy things such as cleaning the ink nozzles and aligning the print head. See your printer reference manual for directions.

Print Quality
- ⊙ Best
- ○ Normal
- ○ Fast

Here's what you've already done by this step:

- You have chosen an inspiration image.
- You've gotten your image into the computer and found it again in the computer.
- You've edited the image (this may not always be necessary).
- And you have some printer fabric sheets (prepared or purchased).

All that remains is to put a fabric sheet into the printer, and print.

STOP! Are you ready to print on fabric?

Your printer is most likely now set up to print on paper, at a middle-quality level. Let's get it ready to print on fabric, at a high quality level. To do that, we must change your printer settings.

Changing Your Printer Settings

Your printer will probably let you choose "good," "better" or "best" (or something comparable) for quality. In general, one setting less than the best allows the printer to put enough ink onto the fabric. You may want to experiment with these settings by printing on paper first before putting your fabric sheet into the printer.

But you'll also be able to choose what type of paper you're printing on. (Yes, you're going to print on fabric, not paper, but you will probably not see "fabric" as a choice.) Different printers will offer different options. You may need to make a best guess at first.

For example, suppose your printer's list of paper choices looks like the one shown here.

You can eliminate anything that says "gloss," since our prepared fabric has a dull, or matte, surface. On this printer, Matte Paper—Heavyweight seems the closest match to a piece of fabric adhered to a paper backing.

If your printer offers only a few options, Plain Paper may be your best choice.

The important thing is that, when getting ready to print on fabric, you can change the settings of your printer from the default settings it came with. And, when you return to printing on paper, you can change the settings back to the original.

Some printers have "Advanced" selections menus for printer settings. Don't be afraid to go there. After all, we have a beautiful quilt to make!

Let's see where we change printer settings in Paint Shop™ Pro®. (This will work with most other programs too.)

1. Click FILE on the main menu bar—click **Print Setup**.

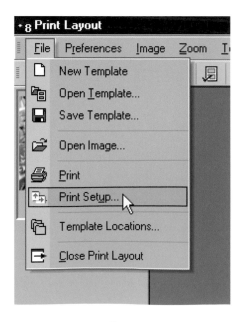

What you see here will depend on your printer make and model. If your printer doesn't show many options, choosing Plain Paper may be your best bet.

Step 1

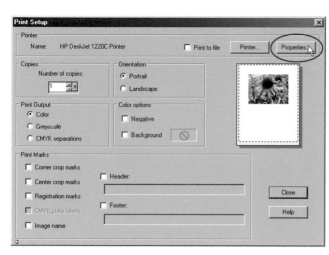

Step 2

This is the printer properties box for the HP1220 printer. Each printer is different, so what you see for your printer may not look like this.

2. Click the **Properties** button. This displays the setting options for the printer you are using. Choose the settings you think will work best to give you a rich, colorful image printed on your fabric sheets.

3. Click **OK**—Click **Close**. Once your printer, image and fabric are prepared—you are ready to print!

4. Place one printer fabric sheet in your printer's paper feed tray—either fabric side up or fabric side down—depending on how your printer feeds. (In general, printers that feed from the front will want your sheet to be fabric side down. For rear-feed printers, your sheet should most likely be fabric side up. If you are not sure, check your printer's documentation or try a test sheet of paper with the word "fabric" hand-written on one side.)

5. Click FILE on the main menu—click **Print!**

We always recommend trying a test printout on paper before printing on fabric. Generally you'll want to let your printout dry for 30 minutes or so after printing, before removing the paper backing. If you use fabric ready-made for printing, always follow the fabric manufacturer's directions.

Dye vs. Pigment-Based Inks

We use two printers in our work. One, an HP printer, uses dye-based ink and the other, an Epson, uses pigment-based ink. Both are reasonably priced, and when we set the printer settings to print optimally on our fabric sheets, produce beautiful results.

The **pigment-based DURABrite® ink** used by our Epson printer is said have properties that make it lightfast for 70+ years. This is a good thing when we are making wallhangings or other pieces that will be out in the light most of the time. These inks are also said to resist water. This means that when water is accidentally spilled on the picture or it is dipped briefly in water, the ink will not wash off. It does not mean that it is inherently more washable than dye-based inks. In fact, the abrasion that happens in the washer when we wash our fabric is said to be harder on fabrics printed with pigment-based inks. More color loss can occur (even after treating with Bubble Jet Set or using packaged sheets) because these inks do not absorb into the fabric as well as dye-based inks.

The **dye-based inks** used in our HP printer give rich color (while not as initially brilliant to our eyes as pigment-based inks) when printed on our prepared fabric. The dye-based inks may absorb into the fiber better. We have not done rigorous testing on this, but those who have say that the dye-based inks seem to retain color better after washing. Because they are not said to be inherently lightfast, we spray our finished quilts with UV protecting sprays such as Quiltgard™ or Fabric Shield.

Which is Better?

Which inks to use depends on what you most often will be doing with your inkjet-printed fabric pieces. Printers using pigment-based inks will give brilliant, lightfast color on the fabric for your wallhangings. If you plan to use your images in quilts or wearables that will be washed more often, consider the advantages dye-based ink printers offer.

Whichever you choose, know that the industries that provide the products we need are improving and responding to our needs very quickly. We will soon be able to have it all. In the meantime, we try to learn as much as we can and continue to love what we do as quiltmakers.

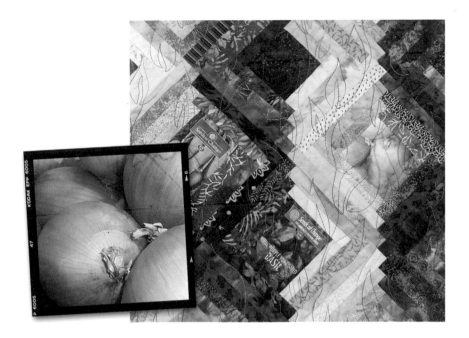

CREATION

Now that your inspiration image is printed on fabric, it's sewing machine time, right? Well almost. First you've got to create a quilt design that incorporates your image. We think this is such a glorious moment (hour, day, week?!), getting to consider just how to blend our photo with the surrounding fabrics, blocks and shapes of our new quilt.

You are now at the point where creative joy begins. Take your time. The process is often more satisfying than the end product. Put your fabric image on your wall. Get a cup of coffee or tea. Invite a friend over. Talk about why you loved this picture in the first place.

Remember, your finished quilt will contain this picture and all the good feelings it brings. We are sure that you are going to love your quilt no matter what shape it takes.

Start pulling out fabrics from your stash. Arrange those that complement your picture around it. Get another cup of tea or coffee. Thumb through books and magazines, considering some of the settings you see there. Stay confident. The only difference between this quilt and any other you've made (or considered making) is that *this one has a piece of magic*—your chosen image—that will guarantee your ultimate success!

W hen you begin imagining an image as a part of your quilt, you start making design decisions. Here are some design questions to consider:

What Shapes Are in Your Picture?

The predominant shapes in your photograph can suggest supporting blocks you might use in your quilt. Notice how your eye goes to the old wheels in this picture. This immediately suggests *Dresden Plate* type blocks. But after a while the fence in the background may also catch your eye. So *Rail Fence* blocks come to mind. How about both?

Study your picture, then determine which shapes are predominant. This picture has strong circle shapes (the wheels) as well as strong horizontal and vertical lines (the fence).

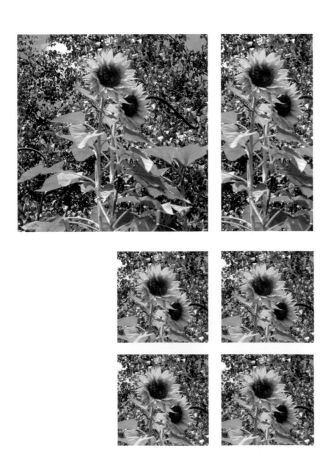

How Will You Use It?

Will the photo become one block, part of a block, or an appliqué? The same picture can be used large or small—cropped or not—yielding a variety of fabric pieces for your quilt. See how these three shapes, all cropped from the same original sunflower photo, suggest lots of possibilities. One of the larger blocks could become a focal point block. The smaller blocks could be scattered throughout the quilt. Are you up to fussy cutting one of the smaller sunflowers?

You can use the same photo in many ways, large or small. On page 103 we'll show you how to crop—this lets you cut out exactly the portion of the photo you want and "discard" the rest.

One Photo or Many?

Will you use one photo, several, or many? Using many pictures is often more difficult than using just one, if you wish to avoid the "bulletin board" syndrome. Finding a common denominator, such as shape or color, is a good way to integrate a variety of pictures into the overall quilt design. For example, in *Your Own Quilted Flower Garden*, we used sixteen photos of different flowers. To tie them together, we made them all the same shape (a small square to fit the block center) and repeated the colors of green and white in the fabrics surrounding the photos.

Your Own Quilted Flower Garden

Detail, showing a flower photo used in the center of a block.

Distinct or Blended?

Will the photo remain distinct or blend with surrounding fabrics? Much of our work is about blending our photograph into the surrounding blocks and fabrics. This is often easy, because of the incredible variety of fabrics available. And no wonder. After all, fabric designers are inspired by the same world that inspires your photos. Look at this segment of the *Canyon* quilt. Do you recognize the fabrics in the half-square-triangle block? We are constantly astounded at how easily we can find wonderful blending fabrics like these.

Here's a detail from our Canyon *quilt. It's fun to blend your photos and fabric so closely that it becomes hard to tell "what is photo and what is fabric?" Sometimes our goal is to make you almost get your nose right into the real quilt to tell.*

What Mood Should the Quilt Reflect?

These four photographs suggest different moods to us. Fabrics also have their own mood or feeling. When you're looking for something to spark a design idea, try asking yourself, *"What kind of fabric immediately comes to mind when I look at this picture?"* Plaid, gingham checks, batik, novelty? Finding just one fabric that seems to match your photo's mood can set you off on an interesting quilt-designing direction.

We'll talk more about selecting fabric to match your photo's mood later, in the Fabric Selection section starting on page 49.

What Quilt Setting Works Best?

Answering the *"What quilt setting is best for my photo"* question can be the most difficult, yet the most fun. Remember, your photo is only a part of your quilt. Our goal is always to create a quilt inspired by and incorporating a photo—a quilt that would still be beautiful without the photo. If this is your goal too, try the exercises below when thinking of quilt settings.

The window panes in this photo suggested Nine-Patch *blocks for our* Harlow Farms Pumpkin Window *quilt.*

Exercises to Try

• As you look at quilt books and magazines, notice the settings used by quilt artists. Think about your photo. Ask yourself how you would use your photo in a similar setting.

• Place a paper printout of your photo on a larger piece of paper and sketch lines extending out from the picture. (See *Once in a Blue Moon* on page 90.) What blocks or shapes do these lines begin suggesting?

• If you have Electric Quilt™ 5 design software, import your photograph into EQ5 and see how it works in a variety of quilt and block settings. This method gives you endless possible arrangements for your picture. (For importing steps, see "Importing Pictures" on page 162 of the *EQ5 Design Cookbook* which comes with EQ5.) To see how we used EQ5 in designing our Harlow Farms quilts, see *Tech*nique 2 on page 68.

• Place your photo on your design wall and get to work on other projects. Your new work may inspire a way of working with your photo. New thoughts often come when you lay a problem or question aside for a while.

OUR CREATIVE PROCESS

As much as we work well together, we approach the creation and design of our quilts very differently. Follow each of us through the process that begins with a photograph.

Cheryl's Approach to the
Apple Blossom Quilt

I put the picture or pictures I'm working with on my design wall, get a cup of tea, and sit in my rocking chair opposite the wall, just looking. I don't try to come to any decisions. I simply look, "absorbing" the picture. It's usually the colors that attract me most.

Take the *Apple Blossom* quilt picture. What kind of feeling did I get looking at that picture? First, I *loved* it. The apple tree blooms for a very short time in our New Hampshire spring, when it's still chilly outside. So I have many pictures of summer blooming flowers—Clematis, Daylilies and Roses—but only a few apple blossoms.

Cheryl in her studio.

The picture reminded me of a time when days begin getting longer and warmer, and I can soon be outside in my garden. I love to close my eyes in the warm spring sun, smell the earth and air, and listen to birds rustling about. (Of course, New Hampshire in springtime also brings black flies so horrible that you can't really spend long moments outside, enjoying these wondrous things.)

So my apple blossom photo brought this all to mind as I sat in my rocking chair looking at my design wall. And this is the feeling I wanted my finished quilt to convey.

Apple blossoms photo

When I printed the larger picture of the apple blossom, I had enough room on my fabric sheet to fit on three smaller pictures each 2 1/2". I used these small pictures as the centers for three of the Log Cabin *blocks. The lightest and darkest green logs are silk.*

My first idea was to create a vertical, three-picture piece. I wanted to surround my apple blossoms with small, *Nine-Patch* mosaic-looking blocks, sprinkling lighter creams and greens among darker greens to browns.

I made some *Nine-Patch* blocks to arrange around my pictures. But I wasn't happy with the results. So I set aside this project to work on something else. (I leave these unfinished projects on my design wall; watch them, and wait.)

While working on something else, I brought out some fabrics. By chance, they blended perfectly with the apple blossom pictures—so perfectly they didn't really need to be cut and pieced at all! But...that's no fun! So, back to studying my apple blossom pictures.

The picture's background is in subtle shades of light and dark greens and browns. The photo's light and dark sides, running diagonally across, suggested a *Log Cabin* block. Since the picture didn't have much contrast, I mimicked this in the fabrics, choosing two batiks close in value. To define the lighter and darker sides, I alternated two shades of green silk.

Here's my finished Apple Blossom *quilt. One large 7 1/2" apple blossom picture takes up a whole block space, surrounded by 15* Log Cabin *blocks. I sprinkled the three small apple blossom pictures around for some added spark. See page 60 for the* Apple Blossom *quilt instructions.*

I'd originally planned to use three large photos. But in my final design, one large apple blossom took center stage. The smaller flowers were not planned, but by serendipity I had extra space on the fabric sheet, so printed small flowers that were perfect for sprinkling about.

Mary Ellen's Approach to the
Wish We Were There Quilt

For me, every photograph I take is a potential quilt. My creative process often begins as I capture a particular image. Watching my photos come from my camera to the computer screen is like receiving a present. I never know what I'll get.

When an interesting image appears I print it on paper. Like Cheryl, I almost always begin a project by pinning the photo on my design wall. However, *I* start with a cup of coffee, not tea.

Shapes and possible settings are what I think about first. I often reflect about where I am standing in relation to the picture, and where the photo leads my eye. I muse about what quilt blocks might extend the idea of the picture.

Mary Ellen in her studio with Once in a Blue Moon *on the computer screen.*

The mailbox picture in *Wish We Were There* suggested diagonal movement leading my eye from bottom-left to top-right. I felt that the quilt for this photo needed to echo this, moving up a left to right slope with the mailbox photo at the center.

Then I spotted a stack of antique postcards on my worktable. I had purchased these just down the road from where I took the mailbox photo. The postcards were charming on both sides—images and words. I flipped them over, pinned them on the wall with the mailbox photo, and just toyed with them as you would puzzle pieces. I knew I wanted to use the photo and postcards together—but how?

Keep your eyes open and camera ready. You'll never know when something may interest you. This photo of rustic mailboxes has strong diagonals and lots of light and dark contrast—perfect for pairing with Log Cabin *blocks.*

I noticed their little red and green stamps. These, I realized, would make perfect *Log Cabin* block centers. There it was! A *Log Cabin* quilt in a diagonal setting. I could use the dark side of the postcards for the dark half of the block and the lighter message side for the contrasting half.

Back at the computer, I opened Electric Quilt™ 5 (EQ5) software and began playing with *Log Cabin* blocks in a horizontal setting. The software's border capabilities let me design a pleasing shape for my quilt. The result was the setting you see in *Wish We Were There*, below.

My creative process includes this kind of back-and-forth between computer—design wall—and fabric. Designing on the computer, with EQ, lets me concentrate on what I *want* to do with the design for a quilt without having to worry about *how* to do it.

Each Log Cabin *block has a stamp center, four postcard-front logs and four writing-side logs.*

For the border, I featured some of the postcard's written messages in diamonds set into rectangles. I cut half-circles into a canvas strip to look like a stamp's perforated edge.

My mailbox photo remains distinct in the finished Wish We Were There *quilt, rather than blending with surrounding* Log Cabin *blocks. I placed a gold border around the photo to emphasize this separation. But the blending, here, occurs in the* Log Cabin *blocks themselves (see the top detail, above) where the postcard images merge visually together. See page 82 for the* Wish We Were There *quilt instructions.*

YOUR CREATIVE PROCESS

You can see that *our* creative processes start with either a cup of tea or coffee. Yours can too, as you mull over ideas. Creative moments must be allowed to happen, and can't be pushed. Let your mind be quiet and open to possibilities.

We hope the following projects will suggest ways to blend your own images into quilts. And as you work, you will undoubtedly come up with new ideas. If you make a quilt that includes an image of something, somebody or some place you love, you will love the quilt forever. No matter what that quilt looks like to others, no matter what others have to say about it, you will always love looking at your quilt. The memories blended into the quilt via the images will always color your impression of this quilt. And, by the way, the passion evoked by your images will influence the quality of your work. This will show to others as well. So don't be surprised if they catch the feeling and respond to your quilt with awe and tribute!

FABRIC SELECTION

"When choosing fabrics, be sure the colors don't overpower your photo. And look at the fabric's patterns as well as its colors."

We both store our fabrics in small plastic drawers. When we are ready to work with a photo, we take the drawers out and put them on our cutting tables. Then we see all our fabrics with the photo at once, simply by walking around the table.

On the following pages we'll show you how we selected fabrics to blend with specific photos. By really studying the colors and textures in your photo, you'll learn to blend your photo with fabrics too.

APPLE BLOSSOM

When we choose fabrics, we look at the fabric patterns as well as the colors. The Apple Blossom, Lily and Clematis photos all blend beautifully with the greens and browns in both of the batik fabrics here. (These are the same batiks used in the *Apple Blossom* quilt [see page 60].) But it's the pattern consistency in the batiks that makes the blending even more successful. We love it! The solid fabrics are silk.

LILY

Here is the Lily photo used with a different collection of fabrics. Here, we chose fabrics to blend into different sides of the photo. For the photo's left and bottom sides, we looked for fabric to blend with the dark, lily-leaf background. We wanted dark fabric, but not so dark as to become a deep, dark spot in the quilt. The photo also has spots of lighter green, with a sprinkling of pinks. So we chose a fabric that also has a dark background with lighter greens and bits of pinks. For the right and top sides, we liked this lighter green fabric that, again, repeats the colors from the photo. As we worked our way out from the photo, we began pulling the colors from within the photo. For this lily, we liked the pinky orange fabrics and dotted red fabric for a little color depth.

BOX OF APPLES

At first glance, we noticed that the photo colors range from reds to orange-reds, with an elusive pale yellow-green of the apples. Our first fabric choice was a multicolored batik, with rusts, oranges, blues and a little green. When we put the photo on top of the batik, we liked the way it blended and complemented the photo. Next, we pulled out other fabrics in the batik colors. But we just didn't like the look.

So, we are nothing if not persistent. We put aside the original batik fabric, and started pulling softer greens. With this new color scheme, everything fell into place. Even though the photo has no greens, apples always suggest trees. And green is red's complimentary color, so is always welcome. The pale limey green worked well here, and we like including fabrics with differing patterns, like these three green fabrics. Batiks are wonderful in the way the patterning and colors vary within the same piece. For example, the batik fabric with the squares has hints of purple. When this fabric is used in pieces, the purple appears randomly around the quilt, highlighting the hints of purple in the apples' redness.

ORANGE MACKEREL SKY

This photo was so easy, the fabrics just jumped out at us. We wanted the fabrics to fit the ominous, stormy mood in the Mackerel Sky photo. We began looking for the fabrics that would directly touch the photo. The dark navy fabric blends nicely with the dark mountain range at the photo's bottom edge. The yellows and the oranges were easy to choose. (To keep that "stormy" feeling, we only used small amounts of these brighter colors.) We finished up with teal blues to complement the photo's upper half. Two of the fabrics contain purples and greens which are not in the photo. But they're eye-pleasers, and we like the interest they add.

PRETTY TAJ

Now, by the time we got to Taj, we were having a ball. The studio was a mess of plastic drawers (a cat sleeping in one), and piles of wonderful fabrics. What a beautiful sight! (We have such happy times choosing fabrics to work with the photos we truly love. The finished quilt isn't always our main goal.)

In this photo, Taj sits on an olive green sofa beside an old quilt. We began by choosing reddish-browns and blacks, but needed added color to bring Taj to life. Using the background quilt as our color guide, we began pulling the colors to focus on first—the purples. Though these fabrics were pretty, and blended well, they looked too dark. To add brightness, we included golds and bright greens. It began looking better. For some "zing," we added pinks. In choosing your own fabrics, don't worry about everything matching perfectly. Sometimes colors a little "off" add interest. And of course, remember that fabric choices are not set in stone. You'll add and discard fabrics along the way. We can't wait to begin working on this piece!

Detail of Maine Coast *(see page 93).*

Detail of Once in a Blue Moon *(see page 90).*

PROJECTS

For the remainder of this book, we'll show you some new ways to incorporate images into your quilts. Our choices include different quilt settings and variations on themes. We used pictures that we blew up and printed larger than life as well as pictures printed and cut into strips.

In all our projects we also chose other fabrics to play supporting roles for the photo image that was, after all, our inspiration.

You'll find a special *Tech*nique lesson accompanying almost every project. Here's where we'll go into more depth with the technology we used to create the quilt. We wanted to present this more sophisticated technical material in context, just when you need it for that particular project. Throughout, we have used Paint Shop™ Pro® 8 and Electric Quilt™ 5 for our image editing and quilt design software. If you have other software, the actual steps may vary although the concepts are transferable.

APPLE BLOSSOM

Cheryl Hayes   *Size: 29" x 29"*

N ote from Cheryl: The success of the *Apple Blossom* quilt is in the fact that the fabrics used blend and highlight with the photo image so beautifully, that it wasn't really necessary to cut them up at all!

Since I did want to use a traditional quilt block and setting, I began by studying my photo image. The photo is naturally shaded along the diagonal with lighter and darker sides, like the light and dark sides of a *Log Cabin* block. This suggested the diagonal "Straight Furrows" *Log Cabin* quilt design. I had recently been working with silk fabrics and loved the texture and sheen they added. The light and dark batik fabrics are very close in value to each other. However, alternating with a much lighter and much darker silk fabric ensures that the furrows are noticeable.

The apple blossom image is very delicate looking, and I did not want to distort the beautiful center. I used an all-over quilting design called "Starflowers" (from The Quilted Rose) for the body of the quilt, being careful to quilt around the apple blossoms. I then outlined the blossoms in white to give them definition.

Materials

This wall hanging consists of five fabrics: four main fabrics for the logs, and one accent fabric for the center of the log cabin block. Two are green batik fabrics that are actually very close in value, one slightly lighter than the other. The other two fabrics are a lighter and darker green dupioni silk.

- Large photo block (1) finished 7″
- Small photo blocks (3) finished 2¼″
- Lighter green batik—¼ yd.
- Lighter green silk—¼ yd.
- Darker green batik—½ yd.
- Darker green silk—⅓ yd.
- Lime green solid—⅛ yd.
- Backing fabric—1 yd.
- 100% cotton or 80 cotton/20 poly batting

Project Directions

1   Print four flower pictures. The four flower pictures will fit on one 8½″ x 11″ prepared fabric sheet, with the large flower placed at the top of the page and the three smaller flowers placed across the bottom. When printing, size the large flower to measure 7.2″. Size the three smaller flowers to measure 2.3″.

2   Trim the printed large flower to measure 7½″.

3   Trim the printed smaller flowers to measure 2¾″.

Starch the fabrics before cutting. Starching first makes the fabric fibers stiffer, resulting in less fiber shifting as you are cutting. This results in more accurate measurements and also reduces the excessive fraying of the silk. We don't always starch first, but when working with silks, small pieces, or pieces that are sewn on the bias, it really helps to increase the accuracy of your finished block. We use a commercial spray starch available in the laundry section.

There are four rows of logs in each *Log Cabin* block. The *Log Cabin* rows alternate between silk and batik fabrics.

4   Cut 4 strips 1¼″ from the light green batik, dark green batik, and light green silk fabrics.

Cut 8 strips 1¼" from the dark green silk. Put aside four of these for the border.

Cut 1 strip 1¼" from the lime green solid for the *Log Cabin* centers. Cut 12 squares 1¼" from this strip.

5 Make 6 lime-centered *Log Cabin* blocks beginning with the batik fabrics. The first row around the center will be batiks, the second row around will be silks, the third row around will be batiks, and the fourth row around will be silks.

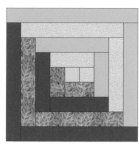

6 Make 6 lime-centered *Log Cabin* blocks beginning with the silk fabrics. The first row around the center will be silks, the second batiks, the third silks, and the fourth batiks.

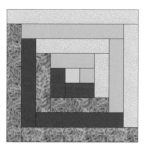

7 Make 3 small photo-centered *Log Cabin* blocks. The flower picture replaces the first round of logs. Two of the flower-centered blocks will begin with batik fabrics. One flower-centered block will begin with silk fabrics. There will be 3 rows of logs in each of these blocks.

8 Arrange the blocks according to the picture of the quilt continuing the alternating silk and batik pattern.

9 Sew the blocks into rows, carefully matching seams.

10 Sew the rows together, carefully matching seams.

11 Border—Using 4 strips 1¼" of the dark green silk, sew the side borders on first, then the top and bottom.

12 Quilting—The photo images are outline quilted in a blending thread so as not to obscure the photo images. The rest of the quilt is quilted in an all-over flower design with green thread.

13 Binding—Cut 3 strips 2½" from the darker green batik fabric. Bind.

Variation on the Theme

Using similar pictures of different size and shape.

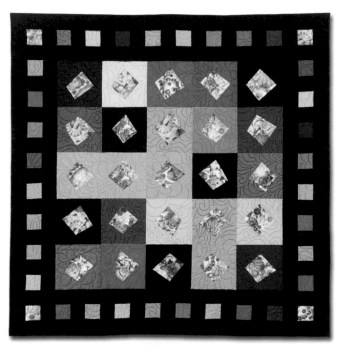

How Do You Spell Chihuly? *by Mary Ellen Kranz*

This was the question we asked ourselves when we were getting ready to make the label for this throw quilt. The photos are of glass artist, Dale Chihuly's work outside of the Glass Museum in Tacoma, Washington. The irregular square in a square setting seemed appropriate to show off the multicolored glass pieces.

TECHNIQUE

Printing Several Photos Together

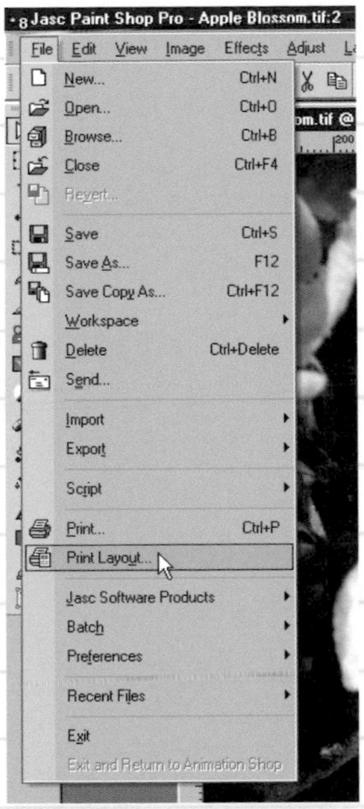

Step 2

Steps 3-5

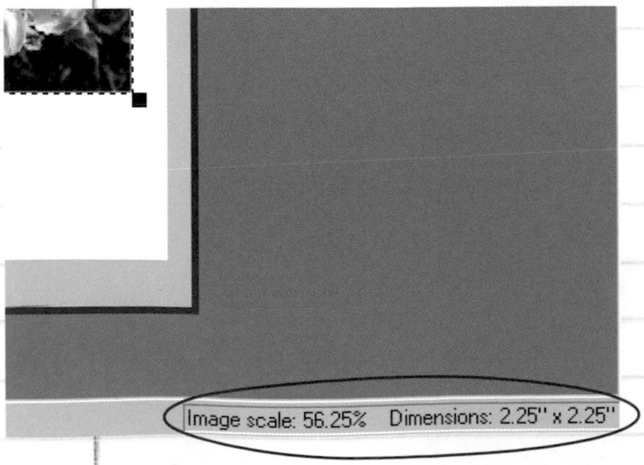

Image scale: 56.25%   Dimensions: 2.25" x 2.25"

Image size shows here

In Paint Shop™ Pro®, you can resize and repeat your photo on a screen version of your fabric sheet. Here's how.

1. Open Paint Shop™ Pro®—click the **Browse** (file cabinet) icon—double-click your picture, to open it.

2. Click FILE on the main menu bar—click **Print Layout**. Your image will appear as a "thumbnail" (small picture) on the left side of the screen and a blank page will appear on the right.

3. Click your image, hold down the left mouse button, and drag the image over to the blank page. (If you see a message asking about "scaling," click Yes.)

4. Drag the black square on the image corners to stretch or shrink the image to adjust the size. Drag the image from the center to move it.

5. Click the thumbnail version of your image on the left again, and drag it over to another space on the sheet on the right.

6. Continue to click and drag the left image over to the right until you get the number of images you need—and can fit—on the page. To check an image size, click an image, then look at the bottom-right of the screen for the image size.

HARLOW FARMS
PUMPKIN WINDOW

Cheryl Hayes   *Size: 35 1/2" x 41 1/2"*

Note from Cheryl: Sometimes the creative process is a wondrous thing! Mary Ellen and I had gone to breakfast at Harlow Farm, a cute, organic farm market in Westminster, Vermont. Of course we had the digital camera with us. We ended up being at Harlow's for hours and hours, taking pictures of everything from wonderful produce, to shelves of pumpkins, to eye-catching product displays.

We came home and printed some of our favorite photos from the morning shoot. I had previously made *Half-Square* and *Nine-Patch* blocks for another quilt, but had discarded them for that project. They turned out to be the perfect colors for the Harlow Farm pictures.

Our personal challenge was to create a setting for the pictures using only the quilt blocks already constructed. However, we couldn't help ourselves. After a quick trip to a local fabric shop to get just the right fabrics to add a little zing, we did make a few extra blocks.

Materials

- Photo image—6½″ x 10″

Half-Square Triangle Blocks
- 4 assorted black/brown fabrics—¼ yd. each (for the darker side)
- 3 assorted brown fabrics—¼ yd. each (for the lighter side)

Nine-Patch Blocks
- 9 assorted fabrics that complement the half-square fabrics and the picture—⅛ yd. each

(Note: Choose 9 assorted fabrics if you want some "mix and match." Choose 10 assorted fabrics if you want all matching "positive/negative" blocks. With 10 fabrics you'll have leftovers.)

Borders
- Inner—¼ yd. black/brown fabric
- Outer—¾ yd. a different black/brown fabric
- Backing—1¼ yd.
- Binding—⅓ yd.
- 100% cotton or 80 cotton/20 poly batting

Cutting and Assembly

Half-Square Triangles
Make 10 *Half-Square* triangle blocks:

1 Cut 5 squares 7½″ x 7½″ from the assorted brown fabrics.

2 Cut 5 squares 7½″ x 7½″ from the assorted black/brown fabrics.

3 Cut each square diagonally once.

4 Sew pairs of triangles together, pairing browns with darker black/browns.

5 Using a bias square ruler, trim the *Half-Square* triangle blocks to 6½″.

Nine Patches
Make 9 *Nine-Patch* blocks. Each *Nine-Patch* block consists of two fabrics.

6 Cut 2½″ strips from an assortment of 9 (or 10) light, medium and dark fabrics.

7   Crosscut the strips into 8″ lengths.

8   Choose 2 colors. Take 2 pieces of one color and 1 piece of the other. (For example: brown/gold/brown.) Sew together to make a strip set.

9   Repeat to make another strip set, beginning with the opposite color. (For example: gold/brown/gold.)

10 Cut each set of strips crosswise into $2^{1}/2$″ units.

11 Sew them together to form two opposing blocks. Repeat to make a total of 9 blocks.

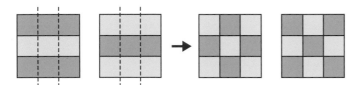

When the window picture is placed in position it takes the full block space of a *Nine-Patch* plus a portion of a *Half-Square*.

12 Arrange your blocks in the finished pattern.

13 Cut your window picture to measure $6^{1}/2$″ x 10″, keeping in mind that there is a $^{1}/4$″ seam all around.

14 Cut the displaced *Half-Square* block to measure $6^{1}/2$″ x 3″. (Measure from the edge that shows.)

15 Sew the portion of the *Half-Square* block to the top of the window picture.

16 Sew the blocks together vertically. You will have 4 rows consisting of 5 blocks each.

17 Sew the 4 rows together.

Borders

18 Cut 4 strips $1^{1}/4$″ from the inner border fabric. Sew the side borders onto the quilt top. Sew the top and bottom borders.

19 Cut 4 strips $5^{1}/2$″ from the outer border fabric. Sew the side borders onto the quilt top. Sew the top and bottom borders onto the quilt top.

Binding

20 Cut 4 strips $2^{1}/2$″ from the binding fabric.

21 Quilt and bind the quilt.

Variations on the Theme

Using a single photo as the focus.

Pumpkin Patch *by Cheryl Hayes*

We were so happy and having so much fun, we kept sewing!

Pumpkin Pie *by Cheryl Hayes*

The Harlow Farm Series

The Harlow Farm series speaks of the special crispness of Autumn's fresh cool air after a hot summer season. Autumn's colors are browns, golds, rusts and reds. Once again, our photos do the work for us, capturing Mother Nature's exquisite color combinations! In *Harlow Farms Pumpkin Window*, the colors of the *Half-Squares* and the *Nine-Patches* echo the outdoor colors seen through the window. We surrounded the window with the darker sides of the *Half-Squares*, to give the illusion of shadows being cast by the window frame. We chose fabric textures to echo the patterns of Nature—flower and leaf designs in browns and blacks. A bit of green in the *Nine-Patches* pays tribute to the end of green grasses for the season.

Harlow Farm Series *by Mary Ellen Kranz*

After working on the individual Harlow Farm *compositions, we were ready to expand and combine three of the smaller compositions into one large piece. Working in a larger format gave us the opportunity to play with light and dark areas, as seen in the lower-left and lower-center right of the quilt.*

Mountain Harvest *by Louie Hughes*

Our friend, Louie Hughes, was teaching a "Slash and Shuffle" quilting class and was inspired by the colors of this photo. He incorporated the photo into one of his class samples.

TECHNIQUE

Auditioning Photo Placement

You can use Electric Quilt™ software to help you decide exactly where to place the photos in your quilt. EQ has libraries of blocks and settings, numerous fabrics, border options and the ability to print templates, foundation patterns, and yardage calculations. The best part (for us, at least!) is that you can also bring your photo into EQ5 and move it around on the quilt top until your placement pleases your eye. If you're using EQ5, you must first change your image into a bitmap (.bmp) file, since that is the file format EQ5 can import. Here's how to change your image into a .bmp file (if it is not a .bmp file already) and how to import it into EQ5.

1. Open Paint Shop™ Pro®—click the **Browse** (file cabinet) icon—double-click your picture, to open it.

2. Click FILE on the main menu bar—click **Save As**. The Save As box appears.

3. Make sure the Save in window, on top, shows where you want to save your picture as a .bmp file. (You are going save a copy of your original picture, in a file type that EQ5 can open. You can save this copy along with your other photos, making it easy to find again.) If necessary, browse to find your picture folder.

4. Click the down arrow beside the File as type (it may say Save as type) window at the bottom. A list drops down. Scroll to find Windows or OS/2 Bitmap (*.bmp) in the list and click to select it—click **Save**.

Step 4

5. Open EQ5. You can name a new project or just click Cancel and play—your preference.

Step 7

6. On the QUILT Worktable—Layer 1, design your quilt as desired.

7. Click LIBRARIES on the main menu bar—click **Import Picture**—click the **Browse** button.

Step 8

8. Navigate to find and click on the folder in which you store your pictures on the computer. Click the **OK** button. Click the photo you want—click the **Copy** button. This brings your bitmap (.bmp) photo into your EQ5 sketchbook. Click the **Close** button.

Step 9

9. Click the Layer 3 tab. Click the **Set tool**—click the **Pictures** tab (it's the last one) on the Blocks palette and you'll see your picture. Don't worry if your picture looks dark or odd. That's because you're viewing it so small. Click your selected picture, to select it.

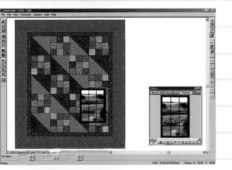

10. Hold down your keyboard SHIFT key, and click and drag the mouse anywhere on your quilt. A box forms. When you release the mouse button your picture will pop into the box on your quilt. Where you place your picture initially does not have to be your final placement. The Adjust tool lets you resize your image on the quilt.

Step 12

11. Click the **Adjust tool**. Click the picture you just set on your quilt, to select it.

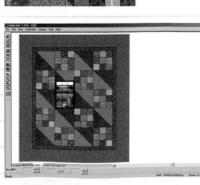

12. Drag the squares (nodes) at the edge of the picture in or out to change the picture size. Or click the center of the picture on your quilt, hold down the left mouse button and drag to move the picture.

Note: To see the exact size or placement, use the Graph Pad. See pages 52-53 in the *EQ5 Design Cookbook*.

JOYFUL IMAGES

Mary Ellen Kranz   *Size: 34 ½" x 34 ½"*

Note from Mary Ellen: One foggy Maine morning, as I hiked across a meadow with my husband, Ken, a spot of bright yellow caught my eye. The digital picture I took of this single Coneflower was a close-up, with a background of brown grasses. When I loaded the picture into my photo imaging software it looked like a perfect image to play with.

The best way to play with an image is to apply "effects" and see what you get! Kaleidoscopes, twirl, brush stroke, ripple, mosaic, are just a few of the many effects that transformed my single flower picture. I printed twelve of my favorites, 4¹/₂″ square, four to a page.

What was the secret of blending the flower pictures into the quilt top? Finding a fabric that mimicked the photo's brownish background grasses. This allowed me to add corners to the *Square-in-a-Square* block in such a way that it was hard to tell where the picture fabric ends and the commercial fabric begins. The alternate blocks are intended to replicate the field in which I spotted the flower in the first place.

Materials

- Photo images—12 squares 4¹/₂″

- *Square-in-a-Square* blocks—¹/₄ yd. green fabric that blends with the background of the photo image

- Foundation pieced leaf blocks—1 yd. total assorted green and brown fabrics that complement the photo image

Borders
- Inner border—bright yellow ¹/₈ yd.
- Outer border—brown 1 yd.
- Corner Squares—brownish green fat quarter
- Binding—brownish green ¹/₃ yd.
- Backing—1 yd.
- 100% cotton or 80 cotton/20 poly batting

Square-in-a-Square blocks

1   Square up the 12 photo images to 4¹/₄″ square.

2   You need 24 squares from the green background fabric. Cut 2 strips 3¹/₂″ wide from green fabric.

3   Cut strips into 3¹/₂″ squares. (12 squares per strip = 24 squares 3¹/₂,″)

4   Cut each square diagonally in half. This makes half-square triangles.

5   Sew a half-square triangle to each edge of the photo image.

6   Square-up each completed block to 5³/₄″.

Foundation Pieced Leaf Blocks

7   Make 13 copies of the leaf block pattern, measuring 5¹/₄″ finished (5³/₄″ unfinished). EQ users can print 13 copies of *The Palm* block from EQ at 5¹/₄″.

8   Cut 2″ strips of the assorted greens and browns.

9   Foundation-piece the block, beginning with section #1 and continuing to add fabrics in numerical order.

Complete the Quilt Center

10 Place the finished blocks on a design wall or floor, alternating leaf and photo blocks in a pleasing manner.

11 Sew the blocks together in rows.

12 Press the seams in alternate rows in opposite directions.

13 Sew the rows together, carefully matching seams.

Borders

14 Cut 4 bright yellow strips ³/₄″ for the inner border.

15 Sew the side borders first, then the top and bottom borders.

16 Cut 4 strips 4¹/₂″ x 27¹/₄″ from the outer border fabric.

17 Cut 4 squares 4¹/₂″ from the fat quarter.

18 Sew a square to each end of the top and bottom border strips.

19 Sew the border strips without the corner squares to the sides of the quilt.

20 Sew the border strips with the corner squares to the top and bottom, matching the corner block seams to the vertical border seams.

21 Cut 4 strips 2¹/₂″ from the binding fabric.

22 Quilt and bind the quilt.

Variations on the Theme

Creating and using "special effects."

Joyful Images II *by Mary Ellen Kranz*

There were so many fun effects to apply to the pictures of the flowers on the computer that we didn't know where to stop. When this happens, we just keep playing and call this a Series!

Joyful Images III *by Mary Ellen Kranz*

In this variation, we used plain blocks (were we getting tired?) as the alternate blocks. There was just a hint of the side of a red barn behind the flower. We played this up by using a supporting fabric with a bit of red in it.

Joyful Images IV *by Mary Ellen Kranz*

Add the possible ways of twirling the pictures in the software with all the possible flowers you can photograph, and this could be a never-ending project. For a change of pace, we inserted several different soft colors into the leaf blocks. It seemed to "twinkle up" the quilt design.

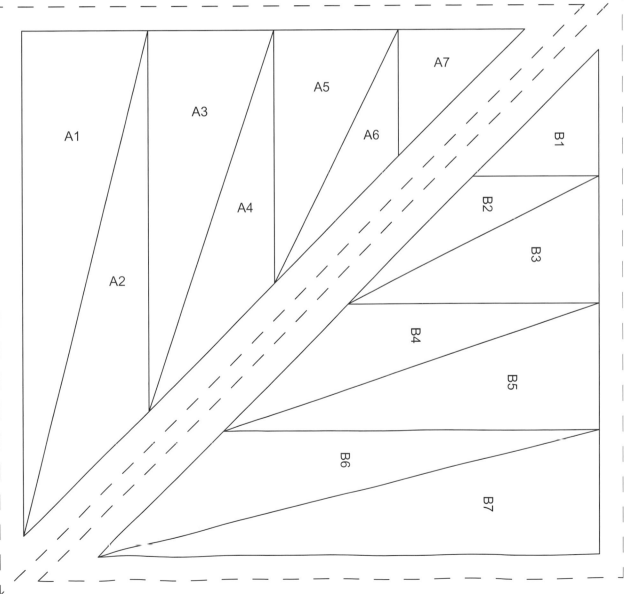

TECHNIQUE

Getting Snazzy Effects

Want to do more than just print your photo? How about adding special twirls, ripples, and kaleidoscopes to your image? Here's how:

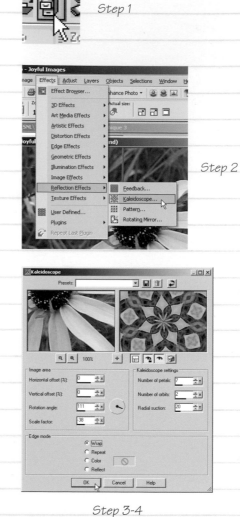

Step 1

Step 2

Step 3-4

1. Open Paint Shop™ Pro®—click the **Browse** (file cabinet) icon—double-click your picture, to open it.

2. Click EFFECTS on the top menu bar—point to **Reflection Effects**—click **Kaleidoscope**. (This choice is one of many possibilities. In some other image editing software, you might use *Filters*.)

3. Now fiddle with the settings for this effect until you get something interesting. It's trial and error.

4. Click **OK** when you want to keep the new image. Isn't that cool!

5. Click FILE —**Save As** to immediately save the new image.

Here are some more variations of our original yellow flower using Effects.

Distortion Effects—Curlicues

Art Media Effects—Colored Chalk

Texture Effects—Tiles

LOST LUPINES

Cheryl Hayes   *Size: 22 ½" x 28 ½"*

ote from Cheryl: In looking at the photos I have stored in my computer, I notice that many are of my garden landscapes rather than individual blooms. In my gardens and quilts, as much as I love each individual flower or fabric, it is the overall effect that creates the magic for me.

I wanted a quilt setting to feature my flower gardens, letting me use the photos as they are, without much distortion. The bargello design worked wonderfully. It lets me blend the photo images into the quilt, yet lets the garden appear visually whole.

I love this photo's lush, springtime "everything is possible" look. The beautiful new greens of the tree leaves and budding flowers promise abundance. To emphasize this freshness, I chose hand-dyed fabrics— very soft and "new" looking. I blended greens into the bottom of the photos, extending the photo into the earth. I chose purples for the top of the photo, using the bargello design's steps to help create the blended effect.

It isn't always necessary to "blend." Sometimes you'll want a contrast, as in *Carefree Delight* (see page 79). Take a close look at Mary Ellen's Scarecrow variation, *Zig Zag Garden* (see page 79). Here she took artistic license and purposely did not step the squares exactly. Why, you might ask? The answer is very deep. She just wanted to.

Materials

This wall hanging consists of two photo images (mirror images of one another) of lupines in a garden. The fabrics are a blending of light, medium and darker greens, and light, medium and darker purples that complement the greens and purples in the photo image.

- Photos—(2) 7½" x 10"
- Lightest green (#1)—⅛ yd.
- Medium green (#2)—⅛ yd.
- Darker green (#3)—⅛ yd.
- Lightest purple (#1)—⅛ yd.
- Light/medium purple (#2)—⅛ yd.
- Dark/medium purple (#3)—¼ yd.
  (used for bargello and inner border)
- Darker purple (#4)—⅛ yd.
- Darkest purple (#5)—¾ yd.
  (used for outer border and binding)
- Backing fabric—¾ yd.
- 100% cotton or 80 cotton/20 poly batting

Cutting and Assembly

1 Square up each picture to the same measurement. (Approximately 7½" H x 10" W)

7½"

10"

2 Cut 1 strip 2½" from each of the 7 fabrics.

3 Cut 2 pieces 11½" x 2½" from each of the 7 strips. (You will now have 2 strips 2½" x 11½" of each of the 7 fabrics.)

4 Strip-piece the green strips to the bottom of each lupine photo image, beginning with the lightest green fabric, green #1. Add green #2, then green #3.

5 Strip-piece the purple fabric strips to the top of the lupine photo image, beginning with the lightest purple fabric, purple #1. Add the next three purples in the following order: purple #2, purple #4, purple #3.

6 Press the seams all in the same direction.

7 You now have 2 lupine photo images, each with 3 green fabrics sewn across the bottom, and 4 purple fabrics sewn across the top. With the photo images right side up, and with the lupine flowers to the outside edges, cut lengthwise strips in the following measurements:

Left photo strip set					Right photo strip set				
1 $^3/4$″	3″	1 $^3/4$″	1 $^1/2$″	2″	1 $^1/4$″	2 $^3/4$″	1 $^1/4$″	3″	1 $^3/4$″

You are now ready to begin creating the bargello pattern.

8 Lay the strips in order on a flat surface or on a design wall. Vertical rows 1 & 5 are your "guide rows." They will stay "as is." Shift vertical rows 2, 3, 4, 6, 7, 8, 9, 10, as shown in diagram (a).

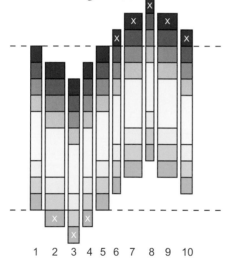

9 Un-sew the over-extending sections; diagram (b).

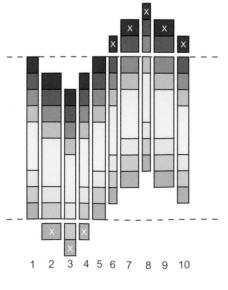

10 Re-sew those sections back onto the opposite end of their same row; diagram (c). Be careful to keep fabrics in their original order as marked by the "X."

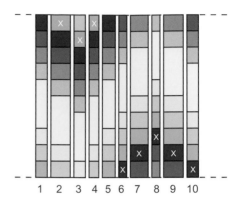

11 Re-press. It is very important that the seams be ironed in alternating directions at this point. Example: Rows 1, 3, 5, 7, 9 ironed "up." Rows 2, 4, 6, 8, 10 ironed "down."

12 Sew the strips together, carefully butting the seams.

13 Inner racing stripe border—Cut 4 strips $^3/4$″ from purple #3.

14 Sew the side borders on.

15 Sew the top and bottom borders on.

16 Outer border—Cut 4 strips 4″ from purple #5.

17 Sew the side borders on.

18 Sew the top and bottom borders on.

19 Binding—Cut 3 strips 2 $^1/2$″ from purple #5.

20 Quilt and bind the quilt.

Variations on the Theme

Carefree Delight *by Cheryl Hayes*

This picture was taken during the summer of the wildfires in Canada, and our New Hampshire sky was hazy all summer from the smoke. The oranges seemed fitting for the flowers and the fires.

Shiny Daylily *by Cheryl Hayes*

This photo is different from the photos in Lost Lupines *and* Carefree Delight. *Rather than standing very straight, the daylily flowers arc across the picture. We didn't want to lose that gracefulness. We accomplished this by placing the flowers at the outer edges of the piece and at the peak of the bargello curve.*

Zig Zag Garden *by Mary Ellen Kranz*

Where else would you find such a creative scarecrow but in the garden behind a quilt shop? This one, created by Norma Lamb and her grandson, had a very quilterly blue and hot pink bandana around his neck. We chose those colors to accent the predominant greens and arranged the bargello pattern to mimic the point of his neckerchief.

TECHNIQUE

Mirror-Imaging a Photo

Our bargello quilts used a trick: using one landscape picture along with its mirror image. (The mirror image is the same picture flipped on its vertical axis.) This means that we had to print one image, then make a mirror version of that image, and print it again. Here's how:

1.   Open Paint Shop™ Pro®—click the **Browse** (file cabinet) icon—double-click your picture, to open it. With your picture on the work screen, you can edit, crop or otherwise adjust the picture before printing. Once you feel your picture is ready to go, move to step 2.

2.   Click FILE on the main menu—click **Print Layout**.

3.   Click the thumbnail image of your photo on the left. Hold down the left mouse button and drag your photo to the page on your screen. If you get the message "This image will not fit on the paper without scaling it. Do you wish to scale it?" Click Yes.

In the Print Layout screen, when we clicked on our picture and dragged it over onto the fabric sheet we noticed that the picture was oriented horizontally.

4.   If your picture is oriented horizontally, click the **Rotate** icon once. You may also want to drag the black corner square to stretch your picture a bit. (We stretched ours to give us a vertically oriented 10.09 X 7.51 image to print on our fabric sheet.) For the bargellos, the exact picture size is not important—what *is* important is to make it as long as possible and make its mirror image the same printed size.

Rotate icon

Step 4—Rotate picture to vertical orientation

5. Click **Print.** (Printing at this point yielded us a lovely landscape fabric sheet.)

You will need one more image—mirrored.

6. Click the **Browse** icon to find and choose the same photo again.

7. Double-click your photo. Your picture will appear once again on the work screen.

8. Click **Image** on the main menu—click **Mirror** to flip the picture on its vertical axis.

Step 8

9. Click FILE on the main menu—click **Print Layout.** Click the thumbnail image of your mirrored photo on the left. Hold down the left mouse button and drag your photo to the page on your screen. If you get the message "This image will not fit on the paper without scaling it. Do you wish to scale it?" Click Yes.

10. Click the **Rotate** icon to rotate your photo.

11. Stretch your picture to make it the same size as your first picture.

12. Click **Print.** You will now have two, equally sized images on two fabric sheets, ready to start your bargello quilt.

Step 12

WISH WE WERE THERE

Mary Ellen Kranz   *Size: 44 ½" x 36"*

Note from Mary Ellen: High from two wonderful weeks at the Quilting by the Lake symposium in rural central New York, we headed home to Maine on Route 20 through rolling dairy farmland and quaint villages. Barb Melchiskey, my patient friend, understood immediately when I asked her to stop and back up so I could take a picture. The mailboxes, weathered wood and surrounding flowering weeds were an irresistible image for me.

We drove on, only to stop again at our favorite antique shop in Richfield, New York. My funds were low (having spent it all on fabric), but I had just enough to purchase some 1920's postcards from Maine. The sentiments on these cards were priceless!

When I viewed my mailbox picture on the computer screen, I was immediately reminded of the old postcards. I knew the mailbox and postcards belonged together. The mailboxes quite possibly were as old as the cards and one day may have even held similar greetings from friends and family.

This quilt combines images from a digital camera (mailboxes) and the scanner (postcards). I used the picture side of the postcards to make the dark side of the *Log Cabin* blocks, the written side for the light side of the *Log Cabins* and the 1 and 2 cent stamps for the block centers. The stamp edge border—an insert made from artist canvas—ties the images together.

Materials

- Photo image—Mailboxes (Cut 1) 8 3/4″ x 13 3/4″ (all sizes include 1/4″ seam allowances). I used a large format printer for my image. You may want to combine four smaller photos or insert another border.
- Photo image—Stamps (Cut 11) 2″ x 2″ red
- Photo image—Stamps (Cut 11) 2″ x 2″ green

- Photo image—Postcard front (dark side of *Log Cabins*)
- (Cut 22) 1 3/8″ x 5 1/2″ logs
- (Cut 22) 1 3/8″ x 4 5/8″ logs
- (Cut 22) 1 3/8″ x 3 3/4″ logs
- (Cut 22) 1 3/8″ x 2 7/8″ logs

- Photo image—Postcard back (light side of *Log Cabins*)
- (Cut 22) 1 3/8″ x 4 5/8″ logs
- (Cut 22) 1 3/8″ x 3 3/4″ logs
- (Cut 22) 1 3/8″ x 2 7/8″ logs
- (Cut 22) 1 3/8″ x 2″ logs

- Photo image—Postcard back (border diamonds)
- (Cut 14) 6″ x 3″ rectangles
- Gold solid (mailbox photo border)—1/8 yd.
- Green small print (top inner border)—1/8 yd.
- Red small print (bottom inner border)—1/8 yd.

- Blue-green batik (border diamond block corners)—1/4 yd.
- Medium Blue small texture print (border and binding)—1 yd.
- Artist canvas or soft heavyweight cotton (stamp edge insert border)—1/2 yd.
- Backing fabric—1 3/8 yd.
- 100% cotton or 80 cotton/20 poly batting

Log Cabins with Green Stamps

Make 11 of these blocks

In general, sew seams right sides together and press toward the center after sewing each seam.

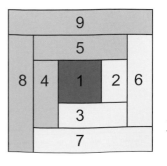

1 Right sides together, sew the smallest light log (2) to the **right-hand side** of the green stamp block (1).

2 Sew the next-smallest light log (3) to the bottom of the previous unit.

3 Sew the smallest dark log (4) to the left-hand side of this unit.

4 Sew the next-smallest dark log (5) to the top of the previous unit.

Continue the block, as above, sewing the next two light logs (6 & 7) and the next two dark logs (8 & 9).

Log Cabins with Red Stamps

Make 11 of these blocks

In general, sew seams right sides together and press toward the center after sewing each seam.

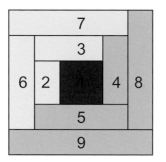

1 Right sides together, sew the smallest light log (2) to the **left-hand side** of the red stamp block (1).

2 Sew the next-smallest light log (3) to the top of the previous unit.

3 Sew the smallest dark log (4) to the right-hand side of this unit.

4 Sew the next-smallest dark log (5) to the bottom of the previous unit.

Continue the block, as above, sewing the next two light logs (6 & 7) and the next two dark logs (8 & 9).

Diamond Blocks (Top and Bottom Border Blocks)

Make 14 of these blocks

1 Place template C on one of the 3″ x 6″ rectangles cut from the postcard-back photo fabric.

2 Add ¹/₄″ seam allowance and cut the diamond shape. You have enough wiggle room to move the template over the most interesting part of the image.

3 Use template B on the blue-green batik fabric. Add ¹/₄″ seam allowance and cut 2 triangles.

4 Use template A on the blue-green batik fabric. Add ¹/₄″ seam allowance and cut 2 triangles.

5 Sew A triangles to the top-left and bottom-right of the diamond.

6 Sew B triangles to the top-right and bottom-left of the diamond.

7 Cut 1 strip 1³/₈″ from the green and 1 strip 1³/₈″ from the red small-print fabric for the top and bottom inner borders.

8 Cut 2 strips 1³/₈″ x 8³/₄″ from the gold fabric for center-photo border.

9 Cut 2 strips 1³/₈″ x 15¹/₂″ from the gold fabric for center-photo border.

Assemble the quilt as shown below.

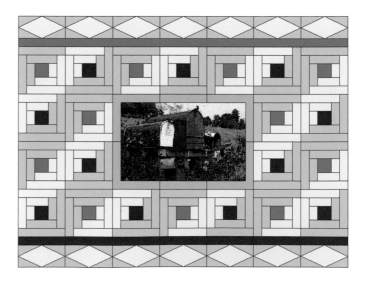

Borders

10 Cut 2 strips 5″ x 26¹/₂″ from the blue border fabric.

11 Cut 2 strips 5″ x 45″ from the blue border fabric.

12 Cut 2 strips 3″ x 26¹/₂″ from artist canvas.

13 Cut 2 strips 3″ x 38″ from artist canvas.

14 Fold the artist canvas strips in half lengthwise.

15 Press.

16 Using the picture below as a guide, cut 1 inch (diameter) half-circle arcs, placed 1 inch apart, along the raw edges of the strips.

Raw edges

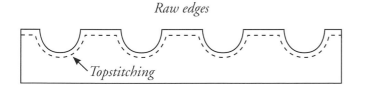

Topstitching

Folded edge

17 Topstitch about ⅛″ along the raw edges. The edges will fray some. If you like, treat the raw edges with a fray stopper. (We liked the frayed edge.)

Finishing

18 Baste the short stamp-edge borders to the side pieces of the blue border.

19 Center the longer stamp-edge border on the top and bottom pieces of blue border and baste into place.

20 Treating the two borders as one piece, attach them to the sides of the quilt top and to the top and bottom of the quilt top.

21 Press the stamp-edge border outward and top stitch close to the seams where the borders join. The outer edge of the stamp-edge border remains free.

22 Quilt and bind the quilt.

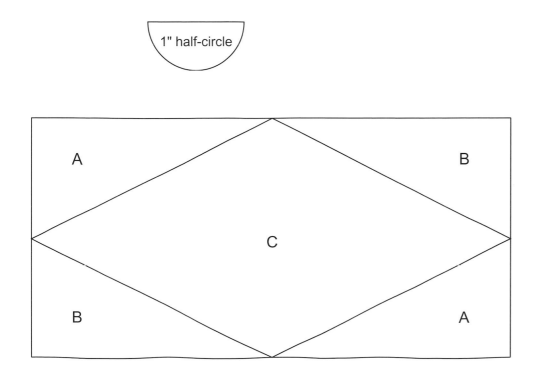

1″ half-circle

A

B

C

B

A

TECHNIQUE
Scanning Basics

As in *Wish We Were There*, some images you might want to use in a quilt need to be scanned into your computer, edited if necessary, and printed out onto fabric.

Even three-dimensional objects can be scanned. In fact, many scanners let you remove the cover to accommodate large items. Some even have a special setting that can make 3-D objects appear flatter. We've found that arranging your items on the scanner glass and covering them with a nearly solid batik background fabric of complementary color yields really good results.

The key to sane scanning is just this—you do not have to learn the ins and outs of the software program that came with your scanner. You can simply use your image-editing program. (This is where learning to use just one image-editing program, and learning to use it well, really pays off.) Image-editing software allows you to bring in images

Step 1—To create our own "sweet" fabric we covered candy (top) with fabric (above).

from your scanner and change or adjust that image within the program that you already know. In the instructions below, our image editing software is Paint Shop™ Pro® – Version 8.01.

Before you begin, make sure that your scanner is attached to your computer and that the scanner is turned on.

1.   Place the object you wish to scan face down on the glass bed of your scanner.

On the Paint Shop™ Pro® main screen, notice the Scanner icon on the toolbar.

2. Click the **Scanner** icon. When you click on this icon, Paint Shop™ Pro® goes out into your computer and finds the scanner software you installed when you first installed your scanner. **Note:** Some scanners automatically scan when you click the scanner icon in Paint Shop™ Pro®. If yours does, then you can ignore Steps 3 and 4 below.

Step 2

The active window (the one with the darker blue bar) on your screen becomes the software that came with your scanner. Notice that Paint Shop™ Pro® is hovering in the background waiting for you to come back!

Now is the time to do the minimum, simplest thing to have the scanner capture the image.

3. Click the **Scan** button. That does the job.

Note: Your screen will be different from ours unless you happen to have the exact same scanner that we do. It doesn't matter. The idea is that we won't use the scanner software except to get the scanner to capture the image just as it is.

4. When the scanner has finished, close the scanner software.

Here we are, back in Paint Shop™ Pro®. The object we just scanned is now our active image.

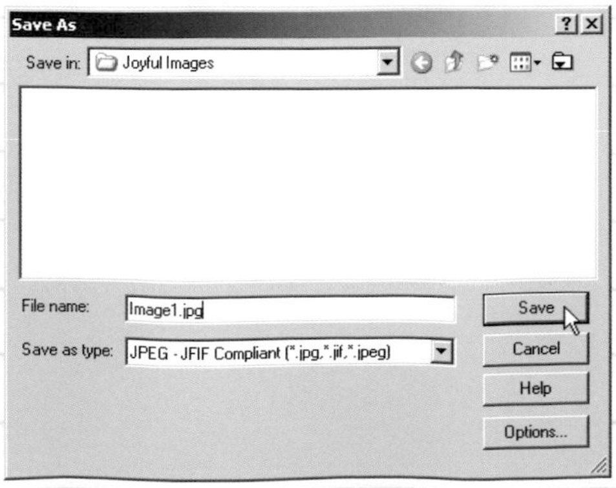

5. Click FILE on the main menu—click **Save As**.

6. Type a name. We gave this image the name *Image1*. Now look at the type of file.

7. Click the down arrow to drop down your choices, and change the type of the image to "*jpeg.*"

Step 6

The image is now ready to be cropped or edited if needed and sent to the printer for printing on fabric.

8. Click FILE—**Print Layout**.

As always, we choose Print Layout to do the printing because we can adjust the size and placement of the image just as it will appear on our fabric sheet.

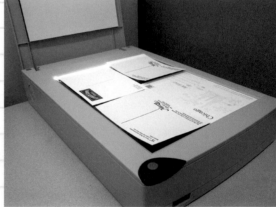

Step 8

If you are like the thrifty students in our classes, you will say the following: "OK. But couldn't we have scanned several postcards and printed more of them out on that fabric sheet?" And the answer is: "Yes. Here's how."

1. Lay 4 postcards face down on the glass scanner bed.

2. Click the **Scanner** icon on the Paint Shop™ Pro® toolbar. Your scanner software will pop up.

3. Click the **Scan** button.

Step 1

4. Close the scanner software.

Here we are back in Paint Shop™ Pro® with our image on the screen. Notice that **our four postcards, since they were scanned in one pass,** are considered **one single image.**

5. Click FILE—**Save As.**

Step 4

Step 8

6. Type a name. We gave this image the name *Postcard2*.

7. Change the image file type to *jpeg*.

8. Click FILE—**Print Layout**.

9. Now you can adjust or print on your fabric sheet.

This layout allowed us to cut the strips we needed to make the darker side of the *Log Cabin* blocks.

Our students sometimes also ask: "Could we scan four postcards, one at a time, to create four separate images? That way, we could crop and edit each image to get just the part of the postcard we want. Then go to Print Layout with the four separate images and arrange them on the fabric sheet to get the best possible layout."

And the answer is: "Yes! You would click FILE—Open image and open each image individually." This is the advantage of jumping in and getting to know your software well. This comes with practice. You eventually will become just as comfortable with your software as you are with your rotary cutter.

Practice Safe Scanning

Finally, we ask that you practice safe scanning. By that we mean **be sure to observe all copyright rules** and regulations regarding the images you scan. Of course, you are safe when you scan in photos, artwork, and other items that belong to you. When you use others' work, be sure to obtain their permission to reproduce it.

The Internet has a number of good sites on copyright. One of the best we have seen is a site authored by Sylvia Landman called *Copyright Facts for Quilters and Crafters*. The link to this site is: http://sylvias-studio.com/copyright.htm.

ONCE IN A BLUE MOON

Mary Ellen Kranz   *Size: 32 1/2" x 38 1/2"*

Note from Mary Ellen: *Once in a Blue Moon* is a wonderful example of blending the colors and textures of your photo with the colors and textures of your fabrics. After designing the composition, I looked for the fabrics. Rather than using one large piece of fabric for sky and another for beach, I chose a number of fabrics for each to add color and texture variety. I thought the water fabric was interesting as one piece. The blues, greens, browns and tans of the *Nine-Patches* carry the sky, beach and water colors to the outside of the quilt.

When I look at this quilt, I always remember the beauty of Huntington Beach State Park on the South Carolina coast. Of course, that memory sparks others of the wonderful times we had there—fishing in the marshes, early morning beach walks, late evening dips in the ocean, and hikes through the maritime forest. This picture was taken on an October weekend during a "blue moon."*

Originally, I printed the picture on paper and hung it on my design wall. As I looked at it, I realized that it was the horizontal elements—sky, dune grasses, sand, beach pebbles, water—that appealed to me. I decided to pull those elements horizontally from each side of the picture with fabric.

Finally, I could not resist replicating the photo's sea grasses on the sand dunes. I embellished my fabric sand dunes with machine embroidery.

* A "blue moon" is the name given to the second full moon to fall in a given month.

Materials

- Photo image—Beach Scene (1) 8″ x 10″ printed on paper (This is used for planning.)
- Photo image—Beach Scene (1) 8″ x 10″ printed on fabric

Fabrics
- 3 sky fabrics—1/4 yd. each
- 1 beach grass fabric—1/4 yd.
- 4 sand and pebble fabrics—1/4 yd. each
- 1 – 3 water fabrics—1/2 yd. total
- Plus enough other fabrics to make enough 2 1/2″ strips, in colors that blend with the above, for the *Nine-Patch* border blocks.
- Binding fabric—1/3 yd.
- Backing fabric—1 1/4″ yd.
- Freezer paper—18″ roll
- 100% cotton or 80 cotton/20 poly batting

The process for setting your fabric photo into this quilt is not an exact science. The idea is to have the supporting fabrics appear to flow horizontally from the sides of the picture. Take your cue as to when to change supporting fabrics from the major color changes in the horizontal lines of the photo.

Here is how I do this (more or less):

1 On the **paper** photo, draw an 8″ x 10″ rectangle around the finished area of the picture. Mark off a 1/4″ seam allowance **inside** the edge of the photo and trim to the seam allowance. The picture now measures 7 1/2″ x 9 1/2″.

Step 1—Using the paper photo

2 Cut two 24″ lengths of freezer paper.

3 Tape freezer paper strips (shiny side up) together lengthwise, overlapping them a bit to form a 24″ x 35″ rectangle. The paper represents the center medallion area of the quilt and is larger than needed.

4 Lay the freezer paper rectangle on a table (dull side up).

5 Place the paper photo off-center to the right. The exact positioning should please your eye for the moment. Since you are working on a larger scale than will ultimately be needed, you can adjust the photo's position somewhat later in trimming the final rectangle.

6 Lightly tape the **paper** photo to the freezer paper so it can be removed later.

7 With a pencil, draw over the 5 main lines that you feel divide the picture horizontally. Stand back from your work or use a reducing glass to help you determine the main lines.

8 Lightly (at first) continue these lines out in **gentle curves** across the freezer paper.

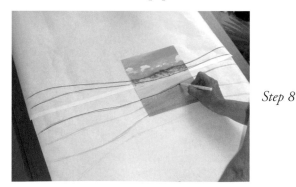

Step 8

9 Erase and repeat Step 8 as needed until you are satisfied with your drawing. Use gentle curves as these will become seam lines which, if shallow enough, can be sewn just like straight seams.

10 When you are satisfied, draw more distinct lines over the curves from edge to edge on the freezer paper, going right across the paper photo.

11 Trace the left and right side edges of the picture onto the freezer paper.

12 Trim the top and bottom of the paper photo to match the curved lines.

Steps 11-14

13 Label the sections around the picture with the fabric colors you will be using.

14 Remove the taped paper picture from the freezer paper.

15 The paper photo is your template for the fabric photo. The shapes on the freezer paper are your templates for the sections of the quilt top that surround the picture. Iron the freezer paper templates to the right side of the fabrics. Cut the fabric photo and each fabric piece from the template adding a ¼″ seam allowance.

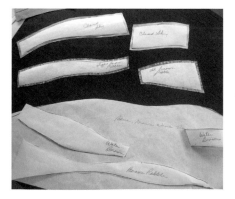

Step 15

16 Stitch the sections and assemble.

17 Square up this center area of the quilt to measure 20½″ x 26½″.

Nine-Patches

Use your 2½″ strips to make 18 *Nine-Patch* blocks. Since these are generally scrap *Nine-Patches*, you may want to foundation piece these blocks using colors that blend with the part of the quilt where the block will be positioned. As you arrange the blocks around the center of the quilt, you will notice that there are gaps on each side. These are filled in with a single *Three-Patch* strip.

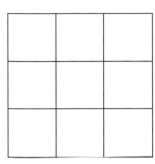

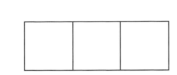

The Nine-Patch block

The Three-Patch strip

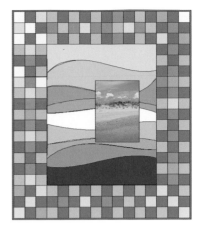

Assemble the final quilt as shown. (Your photo will be trimmed to curve.)

Finishing

Embroider sea grasses on the fabric area of quilt. Quilt in lines flowing horizontally across the quilt. Quilt pebble areas in a pebble pattern. Bind.

Variations on the Theme

Curved piecing to blend the photo into the background.

Your Path with Heart *by Mary Ellen Kranz*

Friends, Carol and David (Irish in spirit) and Kathleen (Irish by birth), often talk about pursuing "your path with heart" in your life's journey. Based on a picture of an Irish road, this quilt is a reminder of the unique path each of our lives takes and how good it is to find home at the end of our explorations.

Maine Coast *by Mary Ellen Kranz*

We always think it is neat when people say, "What picture?", when looking at one of our quilts. The colors of the Maine coast are so abundant in our fabrics that it was easy to blend the picture right in. A bit of machine-embroidery at the top of the green trees on the right, continued the jagged tree line of the pictures. The border blocks were intended to suggest Maine's famous rocky coastline.

TECHNIQUE

Fixing Flawed Pictures with the Clone Brush

The picture that inspired *Once in a Blue Moon* was a rare photo—it was, in our minds, perfect. The beach was deserted. The light was beautiful. The background was a clear blue sky. This is not always the case. We have taken many pictures that were flawed in some way. They had to be fixed before printing on fabric.

Here is a photograph of a sign. It's from the farm where we took a whole bunch of wonderful fall pictures. We wanted the sign picture for quilt labels. But there were those distracting power lines on the right.

Out, out power lines! Clone Brush to the rescue.

To eliminate the power lines, we used a tool on the left side of the Paint Shop™ Pro® work space—the Clone Brush. The Clone Brush lets you pick up color from a "good" part of your picture, and paint it over the "bad" part. It's magic!

1. Click on the **Clone Brush**. The cursor turns into what looks like a brush with a stamp pad next to it.

The idea in using this tool is to position the cursor on an area of the picture you want to use to replace the part you don't want. Using the Clone Brush involves an initial right-click to pick up a color, then left-clicking and moving the cursor over the offensive area.

Step 1

Step 2

2. Move the cursor to an area with a color you want to use to paint out another area. Then **right-click**.

In our example, we moved our cursor to an area in the sky and right-clicked. This action captured a little patch of the sky area. Notice the red X in the sky area where we right-clicked.

Step 3

3. Move the cursor to an area that you want to recolor, then **left-click and "paint."**

In our example, we moved over to the power lines and left-clicked and scrubbed the lines in short, back-and-forth movements. As we did, the brush part of the tool got its color from the area under the red X. The colors of the sky underneath the X replaced the power lines we were painting over.

When the power lines were removed, we cleaned up the area around the sign by painting over the cars and road with sections of color picked up from the bushes.

Here is our finished picture. No more power lines, roads, parking lots, or cars!

ROW BY ROW

Mary Ellen Kranz   *Size: 71" x 64 ¹/2"*

ote from Mary Ellen: Running errands on a winter day took us to the local farm store in Charlestown, New Hampshire. The seed packet racks had just been put out, bursting with colorful flower and vegetable images. Liking the graphics, I started choosing packets—just for inspiration. Cheryl joined me at the rack. Before long we had selected a dozen or more—based only on great colors and shapes!

When I checked out, the clerk commented that I must be planning a huge garden. "Yes," I replied, although, in my enthusiasm, I explained that my garden was going to be a quilt.

The colors and fabrics for *Row by Row* were inspired right off the seed packet packages. The key to this quilt's success was blending vegetable colors and leafy textures. Although it needed lots of green, using the full spectrum from light yellow-greens to dark blue-greens helped make the rows distinctive.

At first, I planned a rather small wall hanging. But the quilt was such fun to make that it wound up being much larger.

Along with the seed packets, scanned into the computer before printing, each row contains an actual crop photo, taken at my local grocery store. The store's produce manager was certainly intrigued to see a customer taking photos of his vegetables. I had a lot of explaining to do in the process of making this quilt, didn't I?

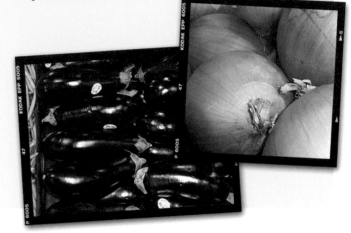

Note: The layout for this quilt as described here is slightly different from the actual quilt for construction simplicity. I've made each quilt row shorter by half a block, so every other row has full blocks. And rather than pieced setting triangles down the sides, I've made plain setting triangles. If I had thought of assembling the quilt this way in the first place, I would have!

Materials

These instructions are for a vegetable garden with 13 vertical rows. You may wish to have fewer rows—but, when you see how much fun this garden is to grow, yours may become even larger! If vegetables are not to your liking, fruits or flowers can take their place.

Photo Images
- 13 vegetable "seed packet" photos 3″ x 3 3/4″ (including seam allowance)
- 13 vegetable "harvest" photos 3″ x 3″ (including seam allowance)
- For the top and bottom borders of the quilt—4 identical images of a vegetable garden row 2″ x 36″

(we printed this in banner format) *or* 1/4 yd. of a leafy green commercial fabric

Supporting Commercial Fabrics
Select your fabrics using your seed packets as your color guide.

Coordinating Fabric
1/8 yd. for **each** vegetable

Because you will probably re-use a particular green in several rows, start out with a range of green fabrics about as follows:

- Light greens—1 1/2 yds.
- Light-medium greens—1 1/2 yds.
- Medium green—1 1/2 yds.
- Dark-medium greens—1 1/2 yds.
- Dark greens—1 1/2 yds.
- Medium green border and binding setting triangle fabric—2 yds.
- 100% cotton or 80 cotton/20 poly batting

Cutting and Assembly

Log Cabin Blocks

All the *Log Cabin* blocks are 7″ square. All have three rows surrounding the center square **except** for the blocks with the "seed packet" photo centers, which have three rows on the first three sides and only two rows on the fourth side.

Seed Packet Blocks (13)

Rotary cut the strip sizes below, then construct the blocks that have a "seed packet" photo as the center square.

Rotary cut strips in these sizes:

#1 and #2	3³⁄₄″ x 1¹⁄₄″
#3 and #4	4¹⁄₂″ x 1¹⁄₄″
#5 and #6	5¹⁄₄″ x 1¹⁄₄″
#7 and #8	6″ x 1¹⁄₄″
#9 and #10	6³⁄₄″ x 1¹⁄₄″
#11	7¹⁄₂″ x 1¹⁄₄″

Seed Packet A

Make 6 blocks that begin with a dark strip at the **left** of the photo.

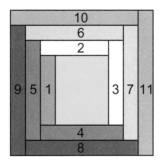

Seed Packet B

Make 7 blocks that begin with a dark strip at the **right** of the photo.

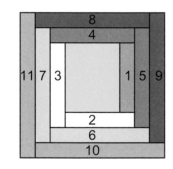

Keep in mind the orientation of the "seed packet" photo, and begin building your *Log Cabin* block accordingly. Six "seed packet A" blocks will begin with a dark *Log Cabin* strip at the left side of the photo. Seven "seed packet B" blocks will begin with a dark *Log Cabin* strip at the right side of the photo. (Strip 1; dark. Strip 2; light. Strip 3; light. Strip 4; dark, etc.) **Work in a clockwise direction on all blocks.**

Vegetable Photo Blocks (13)

Rotary cut the strip sizes at right for 7 "vegetable A" blocks, 6 "vegetable B" blocks. Then construct the blocks.

Again, keep in mind the orientation of the "vegetable" photo, and construct accordingly. Seven blocks will begin with a light *Log Cabin* strip at the right side of the "vegetable" photo, and six blocks will begin with a light *Log Cabin* strip at the left side of the "vegetable" photo. (Strip 1; light. Strip 2; dark. Strip 3; dark. Strip 4; light, etc.) **Work in a clockwise direction on all blocks.**

Vegetable A

Make 7 blocks that begin with a light strip at the **right** of the photo.

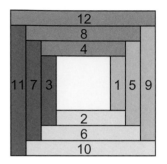

Vegetable B

Make 6 blocks that begin with a light strip at the **left** of the photo.

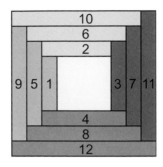

Rotary cut strips in these sizes:

#1	3″ x 1¹⁄₄″
#2 and #3	3³⁄₄″ x 1¹⁄₄″
#4 and #5	4¹⁄₂″ x 1¹⁄₄″
#6 and #7	5¹⁄₄″ x 1¹⁄₄″
#8 and #9	6″ x 1¹⁄₄″
#10 and #11	6³⁄₄″ x 1¹⁄₄″
#12	7¹⁄₂″ x 1¹⁄₄″

Harvest Blocks (58)

Make 58 blocks, in the same strip sizes and order as "vegetable A" blocks. Cut the center square 3″ x 3″.

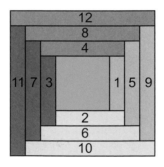

Quilt Rows

Each row in the quilt has one "vegetable" photo block, one "seed packet" block and a number of "harvest" blocks—*Log Cabin* blocks with the commercial fabric centers that coordinate with the chosen vegetable.

The first vertical row has 6 whole blocks. Alternating rows have 5 whole blocks and 2 half blocks. For these rows, make 7 whole blocks. To make the half blocks, draw a line across the center of a full block, add a ¹⁄₄″ seam allowance and trim. The smaller side of this block can be put aside.

Side Setting Triangles (10)

There are 5 setting triangles on both the right and left sides of the quilt. Use medium green fabric that blends with the adjoining blocks for these triangles.

Use Template A (see page 128) to cut out these side setting triangles.

Corner Setting Triangles (4)

Each corner has a setting triangle. Use the same medium green fabric as for the side setting triangles.

Use Template B (see page 128) to cut out these corner setting triangles.

Quilt Setting

Arrange blocks on your design wall—row by row—according to vegetable.

Notice the blocks are set on point.

The blocks with the green centers are "seed packet" photo blocks.

The blocks with the yellow centers are "vegetable" photo blocks.

The blocks with the orange centers are "harvest" blocks with commercial fabric centers.

The white triangular blocks along the quilt sides and in the corners are plain fabric "setting" triangles.

Once the blocks are arranged, sew the blocks together in diagonal rows.

Join the diagonal rows to complete the quilt top.

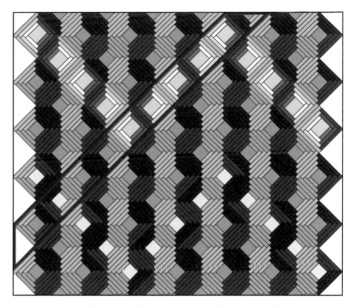

The area marked in red lines, above, shows one diagonal row.

Borders and Binding

The quilt has a simple 1¹/₂ inch border on the top and bottom. I pieced together a long photograph printed in banner mode on my printer. You can just as easily use a green fabric that blends with the block fabrics.

After the rows are sewn together, measure the width of the quilt top through the center.

Use this measurement to determine the length of your top and bottom borders. Attach these borders to the quilt top and bottom.

Some blocks on the edges of the quilt have bias edges. Handle these edges carefully when moving the quilt top into position on the backing and batting and during the quilting process.

A ¹/₄ inch (finished) binding was added to complete the quilt.

YOUR OWN QUILTED FLOWER GARDEN

Mary Ellen Kranz   *Size: 77" x 77"*

Note from Mary Ellen: This quilt is a great way to either "grow" your own flower garden in fabric or keep the memory of your real flower garden alive. I snapped the quilt's sixteen flower pictures in my friend, Barb Melchiskey's, Maine garden. Imagine her surprise when I presented her with this quilt the following winter.

Half the fun of making this quilt is finding fabrics to blend with or suggest the actual flower photos for each block.

My quilt is a throw—your garden quilt can easily grow larger with the addition of even more flower pictures.

A key to this quilt's success was having a number of head-on flower pictures with enough seam allowance around each one to piece the photo into the block.

To download our free flower photos to use in your quilt, go to: www.electricquilt.com/blending.htm.

Materials

The quilt shown has 16 blocks 13½″ x 13½″. The blocks in the quilt shown have a small border around the center photos. If you make the flower pictures larger, this border is not needed.

Photo Images
- Flower pictures (16) 3½″ x 3½″
  OR
- Flower pictures (16) 5″ x 5″

Supporting Fabrics
2 yds. of a light-colored background fabric
For **each block** you will need:
- ¼ yd. of a flower print that enhances the flower photo for each block
- ⅛ yd. of a green color fabric pulled from the background of the photo. If you are using the 3½″ center, this fabric can also be used for the small frame around the flower photo.

Borders
(The measurements for border fabrics assume that long strips are not pieced—that they are a single strip of fabric.)

- Main green print border—2¼ yds.
- Pink border strips—2¼ yds.
- Yellow border strip and binding—2¼ yds.
- Backing fabric—4¾ yds.
- 100% cotton or 80 cotton/20 poly batting

Cutting and Assembly

Main Blocks
The main block in this quilt is basically a *Nine-Patch*.

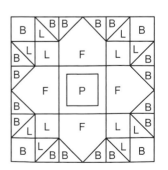

The patches are cut from your flower photo and the background, leaf and flower fabrics.

The leaf and flower fabrics for each block should blend with and extend the colors of the center photo patch.

The one **center patch** of each block is cut either:

- A 3″ (finished) photo with a ¾″ (finished) border of the leaf fabric to yield a 4½″ (finished) patch
  OR
- A 5″ photo that will yield a 4½″ patch (finished)

The four **corner patches** are made up of two squares and two half-square triangles from a leaf fabric and the background fabric.

The squares are cut to 2³/₄″ (2¹/₄″ finished)

The half-squares are made from one 3¹/₈″ square cut on the diagonal from each fabric.

The four **middle patches** are made up of a piece cut from the flower fabric and two triangles using the templates given here.

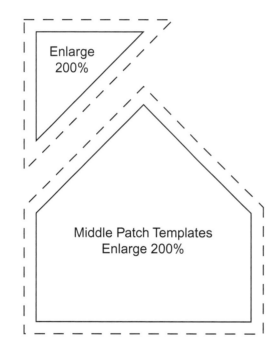

Enlarge 200%

Middle Patch Templates
Enlarge 200%

Block & Quilt Assembly

Sew the patches to form 3 horizontal rows as shown.

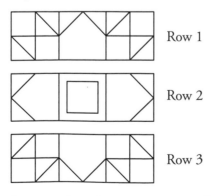

Row 1

Row 2

Row 3

Press the seams in each row in opposite directions. Sew the three rows together. Repeat for all 16 blocks. Sew four rows of four blocks, then join the rows.

Borders and Binding

Border 1 is made from 1″ (¹/₂″ finished) strips of yellow fabric.

Border 2 is made from 1″ (¹/₂″ finished) strips of pink fabric.

Border 3 is made from 10″ (9¹/₂″ finished) strips of green fabric.

Border 4 is made from 1″ (¹/₂″ finished) strips of pink fabric.

The binding on this quilt is a ¹/₂″ (finished) binding using the yellow fabric.

Variations on the Theme

Photos as a central part of traditional blocks.

City Garden *by Mary Ellen Kranz*

A garden quilt is always perennial. A smaller version of Your Own Quilted Flower Garden, *this wallhanging reminds us of a patch of garden that city people often create in small spaces. The sashing and cornerstones suggest white lattice fences.*

TECHNIQUE

Cropping Your Pictures to Get the Same Size

Notice that all the flower photos in *Your Own Quilted Flower Garden* appear to be the same size (to fit the block center) and scale. This is not how they started out! Since the flower photos were taken at different times and at different distances, each picture needed to be cut down to make them all the same size. This process of cutting out a part of a picture is called "cropping."

Cropping can also be used in other ways. Sometimes, what you don't want or don't like about a picture can be "cropped" out. Other times, you may want to isolate a small part of a big picture.

To crop an area on your image:

1. Open Paint Shop™ Pro®—click the **Browse** (file cabinet) icon—double-click your picture, to open it.

2. Click the **Crop Tool** (usually found on the left side of the screen).

3. To select the area of the picture you *do* want to keep, click once on your picture, then, while holding down the left mouse button, drag diagonally down and to the right. A box forms around the section of the picture you want to keep.

Crop tool

Step 3—Select the area you do want

4. To adjust the crop box size, point to the corner of the box, hold down the left mouse button and drag the corner to stretch or shrink the box until it contains only the part of the picture you want to keep. If you need to move the box, point to the center of the box, hold down the left mouse button, and drag the box.

5. Double-click on the picture, outside the crop box. You'll now see **only the part of the picture you wanted to keep**.

Step 5—Your cropped picture

Think of the cropping box as an adjustable cookie cutter hovering over the surface of your dough. Once you have the cutter in place, the double-click of the mouse cuts the cookie and clears away the excess dough.

If you DON'T like the result, you can undo the cut by clicking EDIT—**Undo Crop** on the main menu. The cut-away part of the picture will return and you can try the crop again.

Click EDIT—Undo if you want your full-size picture back

If you DO like your cropped picture:

8. Click FILE—**Save As** and save your new, cropped picture under ANOTHER name. By using a new name for your cropped photo, your original photo will remain intact.

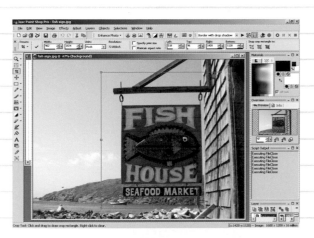

Here's an example—the left side of our original picture had more sky than we wanted.

We clicked once on the Crop Tool, then clicked once on the picture and held the mouse button down while dragging diagonally to the lower-right.

With an initial crop box on the screen, we clicked on the corners and dragged them to stretch and shrink the box around the sign.

When we double-clicked on the picture outside the crop box, we saw only our cropped picture.

Presets

The next step was to click FILE on the main menu and select **Save As** to save this version of our picture using a new name.

Now how could we use this fish head square? Hmmmm.

Cool tip! Once you select the Crop Tool, you can adjust the way it works. Click beneath the word "Presets" which appears on the top menu bar next to a picture of the Crop Tool. (It only appears when you have the Crop Tool selected.) You will see a list of pre-set shapes you can choose from to select the size or shape of your crop box.

PATTEN POND

Mary Ellen Kranz   *Size: 52 ½" x 45"*

Note from Mary Ellen: One of my happiest places on earth is Patten Pond, in Surry, Maine. It is an isolated location with a lily pond that has a dock running out into it. Sitting on the dock in early morning, surrounded by calm water and dewy water lilies, is heaven itself.

I began taking pictures one morning, but found I couldn't shoot the lilies head-on from the dock. My dilemma was how to get out to the water lilies with no boat.

Ponds are somewhat murky. And I am not particularly brave about treading where I cannot see. However, the need for these particular photos overcame all my fear. I waded waist-deep out to the water lilies of my desire. I was rewarded with the most beautiful water lily pictures, making it possible for me to revisit Patten Pond's tranquility and beauty at any time.

My quilt is all greens, browns and purples. Choosing greens was easy—I took my cue from the greens in the photos. I also paid attention to the fabric textures, wanting them to have a lily pad effect—somewhat smooth and quiet. Adding the lime greens gives this quilt almost a luminescence from beneath.

After piecing the water lily flowers into the *Drunkard's Path* blocks, I had leftover background photo-fabric of murky pond water. These leftover pieces were a perfect addition, along with other commercial fabrics, to recreate my memory of heaven.

Materials

Photo Images
- Lily 1—8 x 8 inches
- Lily 2—8 x 8 inches
- Lily 3—4$\frac{1}{4}$ x 8 inches
- Lily 4—4$\frac{1}{4}$ x 8 inches

Fabrics
The fabrics were selected to echo the color and texture from the photos themselves. Generally, the color palette consists of various values of brown, green, purple and blue-black. Take your photos to your stash or fabric store and pull fabrics that blend with your photos' background colors. You can almost consider this quilt a "scrap" quilt, because there is not one definite color placement scheme. I made batches of *Drunkard's Path* blocks by randomly selecting fabric from the above colors. Once on the design wall, it became clearer what additional tints and shades of the colors were needed.

Border Fabric
- For 2 shorter borders—$\frac{1}{4}$ yd. each of a dark and a medium fabric
- For 2 longer borders—$\frac{1}{4}$ yd. each of a dark and a medium fabric (different from the shorter border fabrics).

Cut the border fabrics in 4$\frac{1}{4}$ x 42 inch strips and set aside. The remaining border fabric can be used for the lily pads and background water blocks.

Lily Pad and Water Fabric
A total of about 4 yds. of various brown, green, purple, and blue-black fabrics.

Cutting and Assembly

Patten Pond is composed of 22 whole 7$\frac{1}{2}$" (finished) lily pads (each composed of 4 *Drunkard's Path* blocks) and 14 half lily pads (each composed of 2 *Drunkard's Path* blocks).

1   You will need to make 116 *Drunkard's Path* blocks (3$\frac{3}{4}$" finished) of the Lily Pad and Water fabrics.

Using the templates provided:

Cut 116 of template A from the browns, murky purples, and blue-black "water" fabrics.

Cut 116 of template B from greens and purples "lily pad" fabrics.

Whole Lily Pads

2 Randomly choose a "water" piece (template A) and a "lily pad" piece (template B). Pin the curved edges, right sides together, and carefully sew the quarter-lily pad unit together.

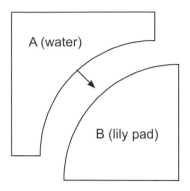

3 Sew 4 quarter-lily pad units together to form a whole lily pad, as shown. Continue until you have 22 whole lily pads.

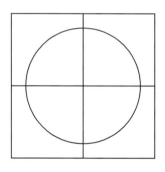

Half Lily Pads

4 Sew 2 quarter-lily pad units together to form a half-lily pad. Continue until you have 14 half-lily pads.

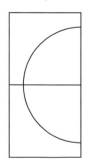

Completing the Quilt

5 Arrange your half and whole lily pad blocks on your design wall as shown. The dark square blocks represent Lily 1 & 2 pictures and the dark rectangle blocks represent Lily 3 & 4 pictures. Note that you are using 2 half-lily pad blocks in each row!

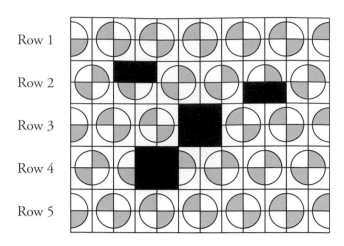

6 When you have a pleasing arrangement of blocks surrounding your pictures, sew the individual blocks into horizontal rows.

7 Sew the rows together to form the quilt top. Note that the second and fifth block in row 2 are blocks composed of half-lily blocks and the rectangular photos.

Borders

8 Position the 4 remaining half-lily pad blocks around the quilt as shown.

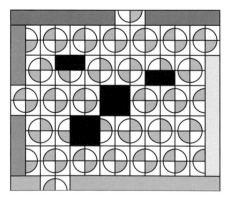

Short Side Borders
Measure the sides of the quilt top above and below the half-lily pad blocks. Cut the corresponding border strip pieces to these lengths adding 2 inches to each for good measure. Sew the side borders onto the quilt top, aligning the lily pads on the border with those on the quilt. Trim top and bottom edges.

Long Top and Bottom Borders
Repeat the above process for the top and bottom borders.

9 Quilt and bind.

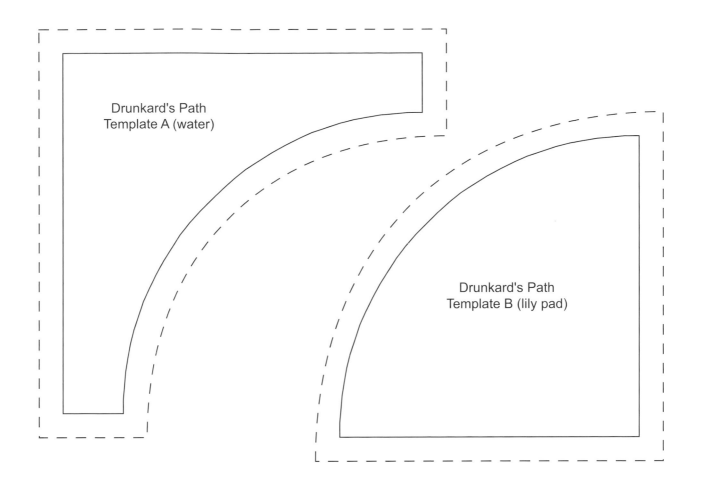

Drunkard's Path
Template A (water)

Drunkard's Path
Template B (lily pad)

Variations on the Theme

Several different size pictures blended into a traditional pieced design.

Canyon *by Mary Ellen Kranz*

To give the illusion of peering down into a canyon, this quilt was designed with a darker area at the center, surrounded by lighter fabrics at the outside edges. With the exception of three panoramic photographs of the Grand Canyon blended into the quilt, the entire piece is constructed of half-square triangles. The river winds its way from right to left across the surface and eventually falls out over the rocks in the center bottom.

TECHNIQUE

Extending the Quilt Design into the Border

I don't think *Patten Pond* would have ever reached the fabric stage without the power of EQ5. While *Drunkard's Path* seemed the obvious block choice to suggest lily pads in the pond, setting them into a traditional rectangle seemed too stilted and regular. The real lily pads in Patten Pond were, of course, much more randomly placed by Mother Nature! If you have EQ5, here's how to repeat the design process I (Mary Ellen) went through for *Patten Pond*.

Draw this block in EQ5, or download the EQ5 project *Patten Pond*, which contains this block.

To Download:

• Go to: www.electricquilt.com/blending.htm

• Follow the on-screen instructions for downloading.

You must have EQ5 software to open this project.

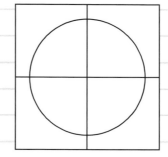

Drunkard's Path Lily Pad

1.   In EQ5, open the project you downloaded. Or start a new project and draw and color (you can recolor on the quilt later) the block shown above. Save in Sketchbook.

2.   Click WORKTABLE—**Work on Quilt.**

3.   Click QUILT—point to **New Quilt**—click **Horizontal Strip Quilt**. You'll see a layout with horizontal rows. I used this layout to let me place blocks in different patterns in alternate rows.

4.   Click the Layout tab.

Make the Strip style: Half-Drop.

Make Size of strip: Width—7.5 Length—45

Make Number of blocks: 5

Step 5

Step 6

Steps 10-11

I decided to stay with the five horizontal rows (default, unless you've changed this in Preferences), but to alternate row styles.

5. Click Row 2.

    Make the Strip style: Pieced Blocks.

    Make Size of strip: Width—7.5

    Make Number of blocks: 5

6. Click Row 3.

    Make the Strip style: Half-Drop.

    Make Size of strip: Width—7.5

    Make Number of blocks: 5

7. Click Row 4.

    Make the Strip style: Pieced Blocks.

    Make Size of strip: Width—7.5

    Make Number of blocks: 5

8. Click Row 5.

    Make the Strip style: Half-Drop.

    Make Size of strip: Width—7.5

    Make Number of blocks: 5

I was now satisfied with the basic layout into which I would place Drunkard's Path blocks.

9. Click the **Borders** tab.

10. Make the border size 3.75 on all sides.

11. Click the down arrow beneath Border style and choose **Drop Blocks** borders all around. I used the Drop Blocks style to give me many options for coloring later.

Set tool

12. Click the **Layer 1** tab.

13. Click the **Set** tool. If you don't see your block in color, click the right-pointing arrow beneath the block.

14. Set the Lily Pad block into all of the block positions.

Steps 14-15

15. Click the **Paintbrush** tool. Recolor the blocks as desired.

I colored the borders at this point but felt the border looked too solid. Layer 2 provided the answer.

Step 17

16. Click **Layer 2**.

17. Point to a border, hold down your keyboard SHIFT key and drag the mouse on the quilt. A square forms as you drag. When you release the mouse the selected block pops onto the border. Don't worry about size and position yet.

This allowed me to set some Lily Pad blocks randomly into the border. Using the Adjust tool, I was able to move the blocks around until I got just the placement I liked.

Adjust tool

18. Click the **Adjust tool**.

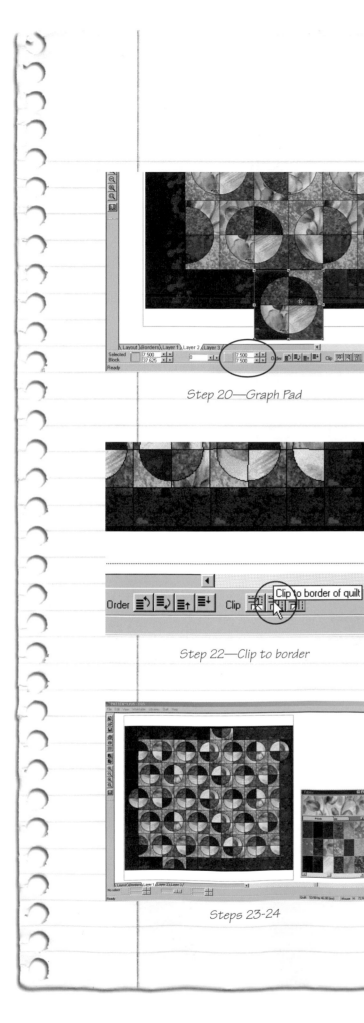

Step 20—Graph Pad

Step 22—Clip to border

Steps 23-24

19. Click a block you set on Layer 2.

20. Drag the block by the middle to reposition it. Drag the block by a corner node to resize it. While it is selected, you'll see the block size on the Graph Pad below. (If you do not see the Graph Pad, click VIEW on the main menu—click **Graph Pad**.) Block size should be 7.5 x 7.5.

I placed the blocks on the left and right borders within the quilt top. Since I wanted only half the blocks to show in the top and bottom borders, I used Clip to border to cut the blocks.

21. Click the block to select it on your border (the Adjust tool is still selected).

22. Click the **Clip to border** button on the Graph Pad.

23. Click **Layer 1**. Notice that the blocks in the top and bottom have been "clipped."

24. Click the **Paintbrush tool**. Color. I re-colored some parts of the borders.

I felt much more satisfied with the random effect of the block placement—the quilt really began to remind me of being at Patten Pond in Surry, Maine!

BIG WHITE

Mary Ellen Kranz   *Size: 70 ¹/₄" x 70 ¹/₄"*

Note from Mary Ellen: This quilt was pure fun from the beginning. It got its start during a studio class I taught at Quilting by the Lake. I always tell my classes that we are all learners, even the teacher. And I certainly found myself learning and being inspired by this special group.

One student asked a question about printing an appliqué pattern larger than the 8½ x 11 inches our class printers allowed. To answer, I demonstrated, using one of my flower pictures as an example. When I saw the computer's Print Preview screen, I was surprised and delighted. I had accidentally checked a print option for "tiling." Instead of seeing my image on one sheet of paper, I saw it spread over sixteen pages. I realized that I could intentionally print images this way on fabric, then piece them back together.

The class encouraged me to try it. So I put the first of sixteen fabric sheets into the printer right then and there. The resulting flower became the inspiration for *Big White*.

Materials

- Printed images—16 (8″ x 10″ segments of one image) (See *Tech*niques for this project)
- Sashing fabric—¼ yd. pale yellow
- Border 1—⅜ yd.
- Border 2—1¾ yd.
- Border 3 and sashing squares—⅓ yd. rose colored
- Border 4—2⅛ yd.
- Backing—5 yds.
- Binding—¾ yd.
- 100% cotton or 80 cotton/20 poly batting

Cutting and Assembly

Set your printer to print a 4 x 4 format of your image. This will print the image onto a total of 16 prepared fabric sheets. Print.

Note: When you are tiling, however, you typically need 9-16 sheets. I believe I only stacked a few—(3 or 4) and then added the rest in small batches as the printing progressed. (Kind of like you add sugar when making whipped cream!) I was just being cautious, though as all 16 sheets would have fit in the paper tray easily.

On *Big White*, (and in any tiling) as long as the printer has a tiling option, there is also an option to start and end printing at any of the pages. So, you don't have to re-print the whole thing if one or two pages messes up.

1   Lay the images out and trim. The 4 top pictures are trimmed to measure 6″ long x 8″ wide. The 4 bottom pictures are trimmed to measure 6″ long x 8″ wide. The center 2 rows of pictures are trimmed to measure 10″ long x 8″ wide.

2   From the pale yellow sashing fabric, cut 5 strips 1½″. From these sashing strips, cut 6 pieces 10″ and 6 pieces 6″.

3   Sew each row of pictures together horizontally, putting a sashing strip of corresponding length between each picture.

Insert a sash strip between each picture in the row and sew.

4   Cut 6 strips 1½″ from the rose-colored sashing square and third border fabric. Cut 4 squares 1½″, and set aside the rest.

From the pale yellow sashing strips, cut 5 pieces 16½″, and 2 pieces 8″.

5   Sew two sets of:

16½″ pale yellow sashing / rose square / 16½″ pale yellow sashing. This is Strip Set (1)

6   Sew one set of:

8″ yellow sashing / rose square / 16½″ yellow sashing / rose square / 8″ yellow sashing. This is Strip Set (2)

7   Sew the picture rows together, placing a sashing Strip Set between each row, beginning with Strip Set (1).

Strip Set (2) will be in the middle, and finish with the other Strip Set (1).

Refer to the quilt as needed. The pictures and sashing should now measure 33½″ x 33½″.

8   From the Border 1 fabric, cut 4 strips 2½″. Sew the right and left side borders on first. Trim. Sew the top and bottom borders. Square up.

9   From the Border 2 fabric:

Cut 1 lengthwise strip 7½″ x 40″. Sew this to the top of the quilt. Trim.

Cut 1 lengthwise strip 7½″ x 48″. Sew this to the left side of the quilt. Trim.

Cut 1 lengthwise strip 13¼″ x 48″. Sew this to the bottom of the quilt. Trim.

Cut 1 lengthwise strip 13¼″ x 60″. Sew this to the right side of the quilt. Square up.

10   For Border 3, piece the already cut rose fabric and sew the right and left-side borders on first, then the top and bottom borders. Square up.

11   From the Border 4 fabric, cut 4 strips 6¼″ x 72″. Sew the right and left-side borders on first. Trim. Sew the top and bottom borders. Square up.

12   Quilt and bind the quilt.

Variations on the Theme

Printing very large images.

Baby Peony *by Mary Ellen Kranz*

We thought this to be a perfect baby quilt for a friend's new daughter named "Rose." When another avid gardener friend pointed out that the flower in the quilt was not a rose, the solution seemed simple. It wasn't. Our new mother friend was not willing to rename the baby "Peony"!

TECHNIQUE

To Get a Very Large Image

Our *Big White* quilt resulted from an accident—a happy accident as it turned out. Here's how to take a normal sized picture and print it out over a number of fabric sheets to get a much larger image on fabric, if your printer has this option.

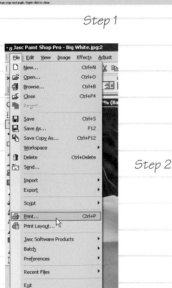

Step 1

1. Open Paint Shop™ Pro®—click the **Browse** icon—double-click your picture to open it.

Here's where you will deviate from our usual method.

Step 2

2. Click FILE—then click **Print** (instead of clicking FILE—Print Layout as you usually do).

The Print screen lets you modify the Properties of the printer you are using.

3. Click the **Properties** button. This will lead you to the options available on your printer. Your options may differ from those shown here. What is important is that most printers now have the ability to "tile" a picture for printing. Tiling means to enlarge the picture and print parts of the image on separate pages, which, when combined, show the whole image.

Step 3

Here is how our printer did it. (You may have to roam around the properties screen of your particular printer to find this option. That's OK, since this lets you become better acquainted with your printer and all it can do for you!)

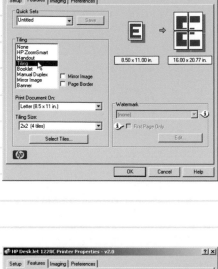

We found "Tiling" under the "Finishing" tab of our printer. It was turned off. Your screen may look different, depending on your printer.

When we turned it on (by clicking the little down arrow), we found a number of choices. One was the 4 x 4 option that would segment our picture into 16 separate sheets. We chose that option.

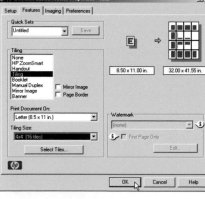

Our printer was now ready to print our one image over sixteen 8½ x 11 inch fabric sheets. This yielded us a lovely 34 x 44 inch image that became the centerpiece for *Big White*.

TECH SHOPPING GUIDE

Note from Mary Ellen

After twenty-five years as a computer professional, I am surprisingly conservative about spending tons of money on all the latest technologies. Experience has taught me that what is hot today can be obsolete this weekend. I tend to buy what I need for now and the foreseeable future. I hate having paid a fortune for a computer only to find myself wanting or needing a new one a year or two later. I find it much easier replacing a computer I paid a moderate price for and feel I've gotten my use out of.

Shopping for computers, scanners, and digital cameras can be a daunting task, filled with foreign-sounding words and meaningless numbers. Don't worry. Your goal is not to become a computer specialist. Therefore, when shopping, bigger (more expensive) is not necessarily better. My theory? You don't really use a computer—you use software. There are lots of intriguing and imaginative software programs for fiber artists. And these fiber-related programs generally don't need the most powerful computer.

The complete computer-equipment package for quiltmakers typically contains a scanner and/or digital camera, an Internet connection and a printer. While you don't need to buy the best of everything, there are some important things to consider when choosing your computer equipment. Here are my assumptions about your computer needs as a quiltmaker:

• You want the computer to be a tool for your artistic fiber creations. **Using the computer is only a part of your work.**

• You need to balance your budget over many fun things—computer, scanner, printer, software, classes, a sewing machine, notions, books and, of course, fabric.

• You don't need the best of every technology, but **some items—such as a printer and your choice of graphics software—are more critical to your success** than others.

If you already own equipment, try the ideas in this book using what you already have before making additional purchases. **Printing good quality images onto fabric is at least as much about knowing how to work with your software as it is with the quality of your hardware.**

If you are thinking of buying new equipment, see the following pages for **computer equipment considerations for quiltmakers.**

PRINTER

(Inkjet) A very important component and don't forget the ink!

The printer is one of the most important pieces in your technology package. When purchasing a new printer for fabric printing, you will want to consider these factors:

INK

Some printers use dye-based inks, others use pigment-based inks. See our discussion of the pros and cons of these two ink types on page 38. Be prepared for the fact that many sales persons are not familiar with ink properties. Most specification sheets posted with printers in stores do include information about the inks used.

INK CARTRIDGES

Some printers combine color ink into one cartridge. When one color runs out, you must replace the entire cartridge. Other printers use separate cartridges for each color. You replace only the color you need for a fraction of the price of the combined cartridge. You will want to use the ink cartridges that are made specifically for your printer.

OUTPUT SIZE

If the images you want to blend into your quilts can fit onto an 8½ x 11 inch piece of fabric, just about all printers will print this size. If you know that you want to print larger formats, say 13 x 19 inches, then you move up to a large format printer. These are typically several hundred dollars more than the smaller format printers.

SPEED

If your printer is going to be used mostly for printing on fabric, you won't want to use speed as your first selection criteria. In fact, you will be making settings to slow the printer down so the ink saturates the fabric.

Tech Tip

Computer specifications today talk about memory (RAM) and disk drive sizes measured in megabytes and gigabytes.

Imagine a kitchen.

Memory (RAM) = counter space
(The amount of room you have to work in.)

If you have lots of counter space you can work on several things at a time. If you have less, you have to clean up and put things away more often.

Disk storage = cabinet space
(The more cabinet space you have, the more you can store in the kitchen.)

If you run out of cabinet space, you can store things elsewhere and bring them to the kitchen when needed. Similarly, if you are low on disk space on a computer, you can store things on disks or CDs and bring them into the computer when you need them.

COMPUTER
Read the side of your software boxes. Your computer just needs enough power to run the software you will be using—and maybe a little more for expansion.

MEMORY
More memory (RAM and video memory) is generally the most desirable component for your quiltmaking computer. If you have to decide between a particular brand of processor chip on one computer and more memory on another, get more memory.

DISK STORAGE
Computers these days measure their storage capacity in billions of bits (gigabytes). Even the smaller disk drives have plenty of room for storing your software and lots of photographs. Even if you amass thousands of images, you will most likely archive these on CDs stored outside the computer.

CD DRIVE
This piece of your computer should be able to both *read and write* to a CD.

DESKTOP VS. LAPTOP

Desktop Pros
- More value for the money than a laptop.
- A flat monitor and keyboard on the desk and computer on the floor can be quite space-saving.
- Less expensive to upgrade.
- Replacement parts are more readily available.

Laptop Pros
- Can take to classes.
- Good in very limited spaces.
- You'll want to *add a "real" computer mouse* for most quilt and graphics software.

MONITOR	For quilt projects, having a monitor that is comfortable for you to use is sufficient.
MOUSE	A real computer mouse (in addition to the touchpad on a laptop computer) is a must.
SCANNER The basic flatbed scanner is enough	The most basic flatbed scanners on market are good enough for the kind of work you will be doing. Some scanners don't even need a power cord—their only cable is the connection to the computer. Sales persons may offer that the scanner comes with free software. This is not necessarily a benefit, as you will use your own choice of software for your applications. (See later info about software.) Generally, features that make scanners more expensive are not that important in quilt applications.* * One exception is if your photo images are on slides—then a scanner that reads slide transparencies can be used to get the images into the computer. This option usually adds significant cost to a basic scanner.
DIGITAL CAMERA Comfort is very important Three is a good number	Comfort in holding and using a digital camera is very important. How the camera *feels* in your hand, at your face, and through your eyes will determine how much you will use it. Hold the camera you are considering. Press the buttons and look at the viewing screen—outdoors if possible—to see if you are comfortable with these physical parts of the camera. Camera price generally rises with the number of megapixels. The number of megapixels for the images coming into the computer is related to the size of image your printer can print out. A 3 megapixel camera is sufficient for producing clear prints on fabric in the sizes currently available on most consumer printers. The camera's Zoom rating is related to being able to bring your subject in closer. The Optical Zoom number (not Digital or Combined Zoom) is the one to pay attention to. An optical zoom of 3 is good for most applications. More is better if you can afford it.

INTERNET SOFTWARE Your "Browser" (not to be confused with a teenager at the mall)	Whatever browser you have is probably fine. All Internet software packages have the ability to move information from the Internet to a specific place on your computer. This is an area where people often say, *"I can download the picture, I just can't find it when I go to use it later."* Make sure that you read our section on setting up a single place to store your images. (See page 30.)
IMAGE EDITING SOFTWARE Learn just one and save more time for sewing	Equipment like scanners, digital cameras, and computers often come with *two kinds* of software included in the box. **SETUP SOFTWARE** These are sometimes called the *driver* programs. This software is necessary. It lets your computer talk to the other equipment, such as the scanner or printer. You load this driver software when you first get your equipment. **APPLICATION SOFTWARE** This is extra software that lets you do things. For example, your scanner or camera might come with software that lets you view, organize, edit and otherwise manipulate images. Even printers sometimes come with extra software that allows you to lay out your images and edit them before printing. The problem is that each piece of equipment may come with a different application software. Do you have to learn them all in order to work with images for your quilts? No, you don't. My advice is to put your effort into learning one "image editing and printing" piece of software and use it exclusively. This way, you will master the processes you need and save time—for sewing of course! Which image editing software is best? The real question is, which one is best for quiltmakers? Paint Shop™ Pro® is a great choice. It has power where fiber artists need it, at a relatively modest price. There are other excellent graphics software packages on the market (e.g., Adobe® Photoshop® and CorelDRAW®). While these are the preferred software programs for graphic artists, I find they have more functions and features than most quilters would need to work with images for their quilts. I also find that Paint Shop™ Pro® has a few unique features especially handy for preparing images to be printed on fabric sheets.
QUILT DESIGN SOFTWARE A tool as important as your rotary cutter	Electric Quilt™ software is an invaluable tool for quiltmakers in general, but it is especially useful when working with photos. This is because you may sometimes want to use an image that has been cropped in a certain way. It may not fit a perfect 6, 8, 10, or 12-inch block size. With EQ5, you can use any block size. EQ does all the math in fitting your photo into the surrounding block arrangement or, in reverse, fitting the block arrangements around a given photographic image.

RESOURCE LIST

Your Local Fabric Shop

- 100% high-thread-count cotton such as:
    - Southern Belle
    - Pimatex
    - Kaufman PFD
    - and others
- Packaged freezer paper sheets for fabric backing
- Packaged Self-Adhesive Appliqué Template Sheets for fabric backing
- Paper-backed treated 100% cotton fabric sheets
- Bubble Jet Set 2000
- Bubble Jet Rinse
- Electric Quilt™ 5 software

We really like to support our local quilt shops. If yours doesn't carry the products you need, they are often willing to order them for you and other customers.

Office Supply Stores

- Paint Shop™ Pro® software
- Full sheet label paper for fabric backing
- Computers
- Printers
- Digital cameras

Some Mail Order Companies for Fabric Printing Supplies

Appliqué Graphics, Inc.
P.O. Box 291
Buhler, KS 67522

www.appliquegraphics.com

• Self-Adhesive Appliqué Template
  Sheets for fabric backing

C. Jenkins Necktie Company
St. Louis, MO 63135

www.cjenkinscompany.com

• Bubble Jet Set 2000
• Bubble Jet Rinse
• Freezer Paper Sheets™
• Bubble Jet Set Fabric Rolls
• Miracle Fabric Sheets™—Paper-backed
  treated 100% cotton

Dharma Trading Co.

www.dharmatrading.com

• Bubble Jet Set 2000
• Bubble Jet Rinse
• Freezer paper sheets
• Paper-backed treated 100% cotton
  fabric sheets
• Paper-backed treated 100% silk
  fabric sheets
• 100% cotton fabric and 100% silk
  fabric by the yard

The Electric Quilt Company
419 Gould Street, Suite 2
Bowling Green, OH 43402

www.electricquilt.com

• Electric Quilt™ 5 software
• EQ Printables—Plastic-backed treated
  100% cotton Inkjet Fabric Sheets
• EQ Printables—Self-Adhesive Appliqué
  Template Sheets for fabric backing
• Freezer Paper Sheets™
• Miracle Fabric Sheets™—Paper-backed
  treated 100% cotton
• HP large format printers

Jasc Software
7905 Fuller Road
Eden Prairie, MN 55344

www.jasc.com

• Paint Shop™ Pro® software

Quilting Images
P.O. Box 305
Charlestown, NH 03603

www.quiltingimages.com

• Printing your own photos on fabric
  services
• Images and photos for purchase
• Mary Ellen and Cheryl's latest work

INDEX

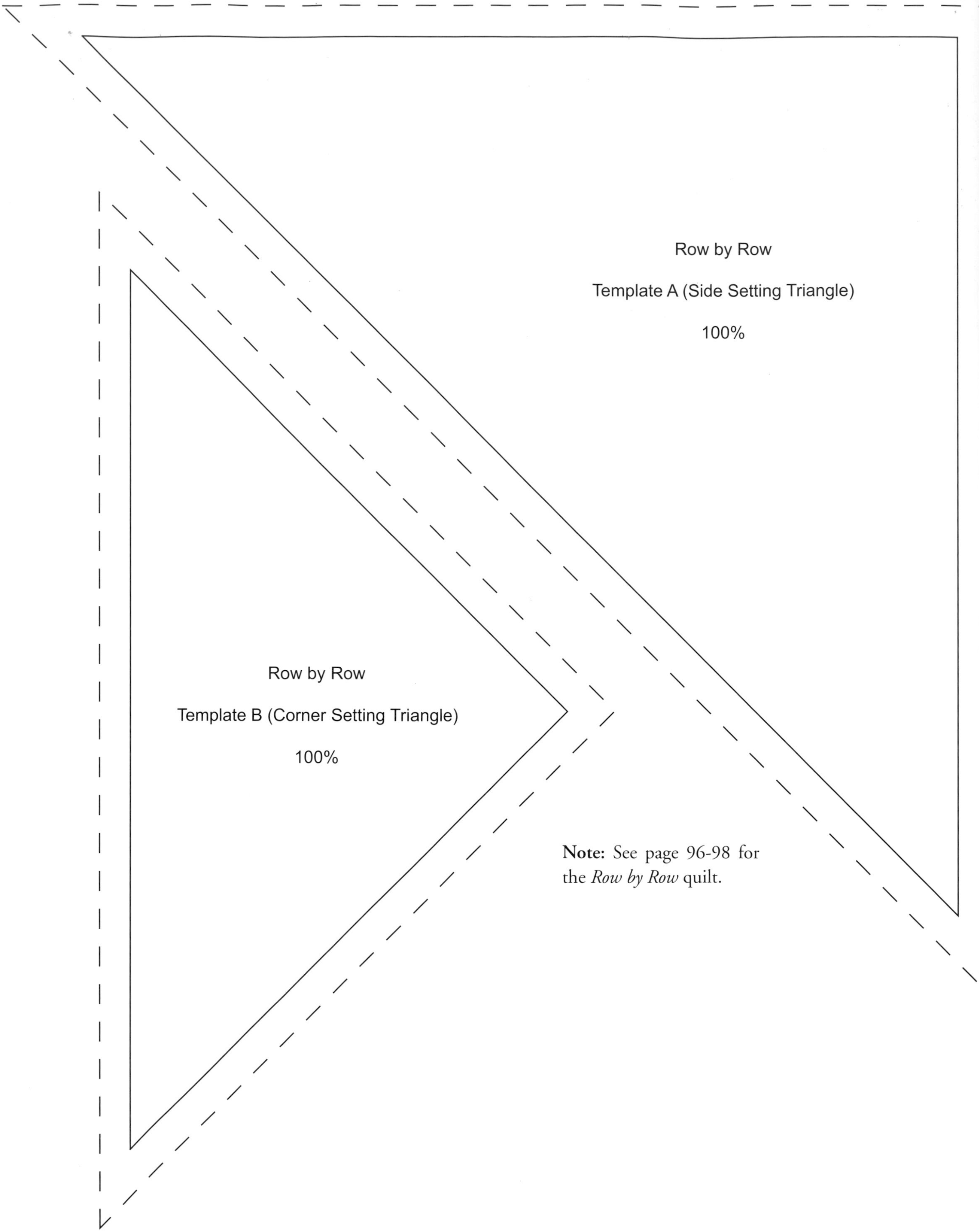

Row by Row

Template A (Side Setting Triangle)

100%

Row by Row

Template B (Corner Setting Triangle)

100%

Note: See page 96-98 for the *Row by Row* quilt.